GOD IS WITH YOU

Confident Assurance for Triumphant Living

YP ACCILIEN

GOD IS WITH YOU: Confident Assurance for Triumphant Living

© 2021 YP Accilien

All rights reserved. No part of this publication may be reproduced, distributed, or transmitted in any form or by any means, including photocopying, recording, or other electronic or mechanical methods, without the prior written permission of the publisher, except in the case brief quotations embodied in critical reviews and other noncommercial uses permitted by copyright law.

ISBN:
Paperback   978-1-63945-010-7
E-book   978-1-63945-073-2

The views expressed in this book are solely those of the author and do not necessarily reflect the views of the publisher, and the publisher hereby disclaims any responsibility for them.

Writers' Branding
1800-608-6550
www.writersbranding.com
orders@writersbranding.com

CONTENTS

Dedicatory vii
Disclaimer ix
Acknowledgment xi
Foreword xiii
Introduction xv

He Is With You 1
When Fears Assault You 9
Valley of Fears -Frightening Places 13
Valley of Fears – Natural Sources 19
Valley of Fears – Xenophobia 25
Valley of Fears – Emotional Sources 31
The Fear Factor 37
How to Live a Fearless Life 41
The King Who Overcame His Fears through Faith 47
Learning to Walk on Water 51
Negative Ways to Cope with Adversities and Fears 57
Positive Ways of Coping with Fears and Difficulties 65
How to Overcome Fears Through Faith 71
Following the Leading of the Lord 77
Saul: Vindicator of God? 81
Ananias, Servant of God 85
A Pathway to Living a Victorious Life 87
Encounter with Angels 91
David's – A Life of Strives and Triumph 97
In All Your Situations 105
A Mighty Help in Times of Troubles 111
A Faithful Guide along the Way 115

Appendix 121
Meet the Author 123
Books by YP 125
Blurb 127

*"Do you not know? Have you not heard?
The Everlasting God, the Lord, the Creator of
the ends of the earth
Does not become weary or tired."*

*"His understanding is unsearchable.
He gives strength to the weary,
And to the one who lacks might He increases
power."*

- Isaiah 40:28, 29, NASB

DEDICATORY

This book is dedicated to my mother Ramona, whose teachings and guidance shaped my life and made me become who I am today.

This book is also dedicated to everyone who wants to be free from emotional and spiritual burdens.

*"The Lord makes firm the steps
of the one who delights in him;"*

*"though he may stumble, he will not fall,
for the Lord upholds him with his hand."*

- Psalm 37:23, 24, NIV

DISCLAIMER

This book contents are extracts from the book *He Is With You, Unleash Your Faith and Conquer Your Worst Situations*, which was originally published by WestBow Press (2015).

Some pictures are original (taken by the author); other images have been provided by Shutterstock images. Excluding the cited material, all the narrative and illustrations have been taken from original sources, and apart from the cited material, all the content in this book reflects the thoughts, personal and practical experiences of its author. Enjoy it!

*"Oh, taste and see that the Lord is good!
Blessed is the man who takes refuge in him!"*

- Psalms 34:8, ESV

ACKNOWLEDGMENT

Like every living creature in this planet, I too tumble and tussle with my joys and sorrows, ups and downs, failures, and triumphs. Through it all, I have found out that my loving God has touched, inspired, uplifted, and strengthened me amidst every circumstance I have gone through. For this reason, I owe it to God and to myself, to share these insights with anyone who is willing to take the time to read them.

I hope that these words could become a source of encouragement to individuals who need emotional and spiritual support, and that the message of this book could make a difference in many lives. Nowadays, people struggle with many disturbing issues that dwindle their peace and happiness. However, everyone can find encouragement, motivation, and confident assurance within the covers of this book,

Finally, I want to acknowledge the role that God Almighty played in the writing of this book. He motivated and inspired me to write each word in this book. Therefore, I choose to honor the Lord and give Him all the credit for this work.

"Do not let your hearts be troubled. You believe in God; believe also in me."

- John 14:1, NIV

FOREWORD

The world in which we live gives us more reasons to be fearful today more than at any other time in human history. There was a time when the only things we had to fear were those that emerged from our routine personal experiences.

Thanks to advances in Technology in this informatics age, we are now more aware of the terrible things that are happening in every corner of the world. The professional media, together with social media, bombards us with grim reminders of these fearful occurrences.

It is in the context of mankind's ever-increasing reasons to struggle with troubles and fears, that Ynes Accilien reminds us all that the only possibility of freedom from suffering and fear resides in a faith relationship with God.

Drawing upon the experiences of many persons whose faith in God freed them from troubles and filled them with hope, enabling them to cope with the fear-producing challenges of life, she comfortably assures us that we too can go beyond the hurdles and live triumphantly in the midst of the terrible things happening all around the world in which we live.

Ynes uses simple language to express profound thoughts. She prods and probes at the interface between our innermost sense of being and the outside world which we encounter daily.

In doing so she provides practical recommendations and solutions, conveying hope and solace to everyone who at times feels overwhelmed by the demands of modern life. She confidently asserts that if we establish and maintain a trusting relationship with God, we can indeed Move Forward in Faith.

Orlando Moncrieffe, PhD

INTRODUCTION

Every morning, we wake up to another day filled with surprising events both, good and bad. We engage in daily activities such as work, school, family matters, ministries, and so forth. As the day unfolds, our lives get congested with more activities, events, circumstances, and other things that could make our experiences more peaceful and pleasant, or difficult and stressful.

The increasing frequency of unwanted and unfortunate occurrences commonly leave people struggling with loads of unfortunate situations. As time passes by, a mix of distresses, panic and fears is what is left in the aftermath of unwanted circumstances and heartbreaking events.

This current state of affairs has motivated me to do something to spread away some inspiring hope for anyone who is willing to receive it. This hope is now available to everyone and has come in the form of the book you are now reading: *God's with You*.

Before writing this book, I asked God to impress upon my mind with the words He wanted me to write about, and I am certain that He heard my prayer. This book contains insightful information that can lead readers into a path of confidence in His promises.

I firmly believe that the contents in this book can become a powerful antidote against many feelings and reactions that people experience each day. It can also become a wonderful source spiritual solace for individuals who are chasing after inner peace.

Millions of people believe in the existence of God. I count myself among their number. I do believe that the Lord knows what we are going through and walks by our side each moment of our lives. This concept of an ever-present God is another important reason that prompted me to write this book.

The Lord has spoken to us His promises of hope, promises of strength, promises of peace, and so forth. These promises point to the same central idea: God is with us, upholding us, keeping us, blessing us, and helping us get through our situations, and this, my friend, is the main theme of this book.

Those who walk with Him by faith will find out that God has given everyone wonderful promises for every situation; many of them are cited in this book. This initiative can empower individuals to overcome many obstacles and become emotionally and spiritually stronger to endure many situations that are typical of everyday living.

The contents in this book, its stories, anecdotes, insights, inspiring thoughts, and Bible promises, which deliberate on several matters that can affect people's lives personally and collectively. Its numerous directives can also help individuals focus their attention on the power of faith in God's promises.

Now that you know what the book is all about, I would like to encourage you to delve into the pages of this book, keeping in mind that God is with you always. So, start your reading journey and discover the plan and purpose God has for every season in your life; be blessed, and be a blessing!

The Author

HE IS WITH YOU

Have you ever felt so overwhelmed by your circumstances, that in your oblivion, you convinced yourself that you were alone and forsaken in the world? If that were so, allow me to tell you that you are not the only person in this planet that has ever felt this way.

Millions of people around the glove have been dealing with this feeling from the very beginning of human history. Thousands of years before the birth of Christ, the ancient Israelites who pilgrimaged through the desert, felt terrified by the Canaanites people.

Then, speaking on God's behalf, their leader Moses, and comforted these people with the assurance of an ever present and caring God that was always by their side. One day he told them:

"Be strong and courageous. Do not fear... for the Lord your God is the one who goes with you. He will not fail you or forsake you."

(Deuteronomy 31: 6, NASB)

Thousands of years later, a noble shepherd boy wrote the beloved song that is known by many as *The Psalm of the Shepherd*. Describing his own feelings, the young Cantor wrote:

The Lord is my shepherd; I shall not want. He makes me to lie down in green pastures: He leads me beside the still waters. He restores my soul: He leads me in the paths of righteousness for His name's sake.

Yea, though I walk through the valley of shadow of death, I will fear no evil" for You art with me; Your rod and thy staff they comfort me. You prepare a table before me in the presence of mine enemies: You anoint my head with oil; my cup runs over.

Surely, goodness and mercy shall follow me all the days of my life, and I will dwell in the house of the Lord forever (Psalms 23, NASB).

This psalm is one of the most beautiful poems ever written in religious literature. It is about the confidence of a sheep in his shepherd.

Wait a minute! Let us reconsider this thought again and ask ourselves this question: Do sheep write poems? No, they do not. Then, who wrote this one? You got it! It was David, the shepherd boy.

As he pastored his flock, he took time to meditate in God's love and tender care for His creatures. His familiarity with his flock led this young shepherd to compare his relationship with the Lord to that of a shepherd with his sheep. This was a picture he could relate with. David thought of himself as a sheep, which was being led by God, his Good Shepherd.

Now, let us imagine ourselves as sheep of a flock. Can we do that? I do not know about you, but I cannot do it. Personally, I think that this type of mental exercise could be a bit difficult for anyone who is not familiar with the business of tending sheep or cattle of any kind.

However, let us keep in mind that this example is based on David's personal relationship with the Lord. He could not have pictured himself as a cowboy, because he was not one. He could not imagine himself as a student because the theme of his poem had nothing to do with a teacher-student relationship. He could talk about a parent-child relationship because in this case, David was the child, not a father.

Thus, the only position David could relate to as a leader was that of a shepherd. How about you? Do you have a personal relationship with God? What allegories can you use to compare your relationship with Him? Who are you, and who is the Lord in that relationship?

Whenever I think about applying this psalm to my personal life, the only thing I could use to compare my relationship with God is my motherhood. As a mother, I can relate with my children as their guide, and with the Lord as my Father and leader of my life; it is easy for me to understand God's love through those relationships.

I do not own any sheep and know nothing about caring for animals and herds; but I have heard that lambs and adult sheep are very delicate animals. It is said that if they fall down, they might not be able to get up unless they are assisted by someone.

When explaining the parable of *the lost sheep* of Luke 15:1-10, I have heard some preachers say that sheep are delicate animals. According to these gospel ministers, without help, a lost sheep might not be able to find its way back to the sheepfold. Therefore, shepherds have to watchfully care and constantly supervise their sheep to keep them safe.

Practical Application

A child's life is a precious gift to those who receive it. Therefore, parents and caregivers must take good care of their precious treasures. Human babies are also very tender and delicate both, physically and emotionally. Thus, they need to be nurtured, protected, shielded, clothed, and sheltered by loved ones and caretakers.

As they grow up, the love and tender devotion that children received from responsible parents and caregivers can bestow unto them can make a big difference in their physical and emotional lives.

Many children who are not properly cared for and nurtured by loving parents and caretakers are more likely to get physical and emotionally hurt, and their visible or invisible scars can have negative impacts on their normal growth and development (go to the appendix for more data on this matter).

Neglected children are also more likely to get sick with acquired and preventable illnesses that could be easily recognized, diagnosed, and ratified by expert physicians and behaviorists. Failure to address their issues could cut these children's lives short and reduce their chance to learn what life is all about.

No child deserves this type of treatment and yet, many little ones currently bear in the marks of physical and emotional of childhood neglect. Raising a child is a big, but wonderful responsibility that not many people are prepared to assume when they first become parents. Believe it or not, I was one of those people.

When I first became a mother, I felt inadequate and apprehensive, and unfit to care for and look after my own child. Like any other baby, he was very wobbly and defenseless during the first weeks of his neonatal life.

I was afraid to carry him, hold him in my arms, and attending his needs. However, I shared those concerns with my mother, and she taught me what to do.

My mother told me that young babies were "as flexible as rubber" and that if I just learned to hold my baby properly and without fears, everything else would be alright. Her advice gave me all the confidence I needed.

Almost immediately, I learned how to handle my baby's needs; no longer was I afraid of letting him fall or doing something wrong that could accidentally harm him. I was finally ready to fulfil my maternal responsibilities.

From that day on, I felt much more confident when feeding, bathing, clothing, and massaging, and cuddling my baby. I gave him all the loving sweetness that any mother should bestow unto her offspring. Caring for him turned out to be a lot easier than I thought.

The days turned into weeks, the weeks into months, and the months into years, and my child kept on growing up healthily. I made sure that he had everything he needed and never stopped watching over him.

Years later, I had three other children and I gave them with the same love and tenderness as I did to my first born. However, the experience I accumulated throughout the years caused my maternal responsibilities to become easier each time around.

Thus, as you may see, I was not born a mother; I had to learn to become one. Today, while pondering upon those things, I feel that my experience has helped me grasp a better understanding of the love God has for His creatures.

Babies need lots of care from their loved ones. Parents and caretakers must nurture, shelter, shield and protect their little ones, and meet their every need to ensure adequate growth and development.

Photo courtesy of the author

Unlike me, God does not have to learn how to deal with us because as the Creator, He already knows everything about us and how we function.

The Holy Scriptures tells us: "*You formed my inward parts; you wove me in my mother's womb*" (Psalm 139:13, NASB). Becoming aware of this realization is such a wonderful thing!

Surely, our loving God cares for us. He knows us very well and has promised to supply our every need. Hence, let us put our cares aside and trust in Him, because our heavenly Father can supply our every need. Jesus said: *Do not worry saying what should we eat? Or what should we drink? Or what shall we wear? For the pagans run after all these things, and your heavenly Father knows that you need them. Seek first His Kingdom and His righteousness and all these things will be given to you as well* (Matthew 6: 31-33, NIV).

Life becomes easier and better when we abide in God's love because He does not just provide for our physical needs, but also for our emotional and spiritual ones. Parents trace their children's paths with guidelines and instructions. Likewise, the Lord deals with us –His Children, the sheep of His pastures.

The Lord leads us through the green pastures, through still waters, to the paths of righteousness for His name's sake. In other words, God's commitment to supply for our physical, emotional, and material needs brings honor to His name, and He is happy taking care of His creatures.

Talking about the heavenly Father, Jesus told His disciples that God's tender care is bestowed unto everyone. *"He causes the sun to rise on the evil and the good; and sends rain on the righteous and the unrighteous"* (Matthew 5:45, NASB).

This wonderful truth has caused many people, who do not have a personal relationship with God, to become more aware of the ways in which God deals with His children. Then, many of these agnostics marvel have a change of heart and surrender to God's love.

Unfortunately, other people are more reluctant to surrender to God's tender ways; they rather reject Him than having a personal relationship with their Maker. These folks' behavior resembles the attitude exhibited by the Jewish nation towards Jesus back in the first century of our current era.

Speaking about said occurrence, John, the apostle said that the majority of people did not receive Jesus well, as it is written: *"He came to His own, and those who were His own did not receive Him"* (John 1:11, NASB). Even though, the Lord blessed them back then, and till this day, God continues to pour out His showers of blessings unto everybody.

Today, God continues to reach out to every Jew, American, Asian, African, and European person, and gives everyone the time and opportunities they need to surrender to His love. Truly, God is in the business of blessing people, and He has filled the Earth with all the resources we need to survive and thrive as species.

Unfortunately, there are still plenty of needs, and abundance of misery, heartache, and brokenness everywhere. Such deplorable situations have turned many of God's creatures into wanderers and beggars of physical, material, emotional, and spiritual blessings.

However, God has not abandoned the children of His creation. He continues to watch over all of them. The Bible says: *"The Lord's lovingkindness indeed never ceases, for His compassions never fail. They are new every morning"* (Lamentations 3: 22, 23, NASB).

Indeed, *"God's goodness and mercy will follow us for the rest of our lives"* (Psalm 23:6, paraphrased). This means that God's promises of providing for our needs and protecting us from evil is the real deal. His willingness to shower us with His goodness and lovingkindness is God's gift and desire for every child of the human race, because we are *"His people and the sheep of His pasture"* (Psalm 100:2, NASB).

Appeal

Though we are still pilgrims and wanderers in the journey of this life, God still cares for us, and He always will. He wants us to be happy in this life and the one to come. Therefore, He is always by our side and provides for our every need.

The Lord has promised that someday, when all is set and done, He will come again to take us to His holy place. On that day, we will join the shepherd boy and sing: "In the house of the Lord I will live forever"

I believe the Word and embrace God's promises, how about you? Do you believe it? If so, be confident in the midst of your struggles and live like sheep which depend on their shepherds. Only then, you will know by experience that the Good Shepherd is more than willing and able to take care of you all the days of your life. Dwell in the assurance of God's promises and embrace the peace that your good Father has in store for you.

Photo courtesy of the author

WHEN FEARS ASSAULT YOU

Psalm 27 is one of my secret weapons to fight distresses and fears. One of its verses says: *"The Lord is my light and my salvation—whom shall I fear? The Lord is the strength of my life—whom shall I be afraid?"*
(Psalm 27:1, KJV)

These verses are like fountains of hope, which spring out confident assurance for a better future. Sadly, people who claim that they fear nothing cannot receive the benefits of these blessed words because they have "no need" of savior or salvation.

Have you ever been approached by one of those folks? What is your take on their statements? Would you really believe them? Is it possible that they are right? Can there really be a person on Earth who is completely fearless?

I hardly believe that such person exists; yet, since everything is possible, perhaps there is there is someone out there who really fears nothing. However, I still believe that the likelihood of not finding such person is even greater. Surely, life could be like a bumpy ride where people are likely to come across different obstacles, some of which could be quite frightening.

Life's obstacles could come in the shapes of hurdles or difficulties that people encounter along their journeys through this earth. For this reason, I believe that it is for everyone to understand the concepts and mechanisms of fears. To that end, let us scrutinize the following realistic situations.

People who live with jealous, abusive, and mentally unstable loved ones are typically prone to feel afraid of being physical or emotionally hurt anytime.

People have lost loved ones are likely to fear the loneliness of the place in which they live.

People are unprepared are usually afraid of failing.

These are just a few mere examples of situations that could cause fear to assault the lives of many people. Of course, nobody likes living in fear. However, the journey of life is plentiful with all kind of pleasant, unpleasant, daunting, and frightening situations, and everybody gets a share of them.

The end result of these situations could translate into happiness, contentment, and peace, but could also spur despairs, anxieties, and fears. Certainly, there are many brave and bold people out there; but the truth is that for as long as we live in this world, there will always be some reason to become apprehensive or fearful of something.

Fear is a feeling that is common to everybody. This sentiment made its entrance into this world in the beginning, in the Garden of Eden, where our foreparents hid from the presence of God, fearing the consequences of their disobedience. Since then, everybody has had to deal with this negative emotion in one way or another.

Practical Application

Individuals may ponder on the possible reasons or source(s) of fears, and whether these feelings have reasonable grounds to exist. In time, many folks become aware of things and factors that could be involved in their genesis of fears.

People's fears may arise from almost anything, and they are linked to places, people, animals, things, and even feelings. Each source plays a pivotal role in coping with the fears it evokes. Hence, it is important to become aware of any frightening thing that may disturb one's mental peace. Likewise, understanding what lies beneath their fearful feelings is another key to open the vaults of solutions to help individuals deal with this type of negative emotion called fear.

Appeal

People who believe in God can fight their fears through faith and conquer them. The more they trust in God, the safer they will feel. They will rest under the shadow of the Almighty (Psalm 91:1.2) and will claim His comforting promises.

The Word of the Lord: *"Do not fear for I am with you… I will strengthen you, surely I will help you"* (Isaiah 41:10, NASB) will resonate in their minds and will cast away all fears. Do you believe this?

*"Do not fear, for I am with you;
Do not be afraid, for I am your God.
I will strengthen you, I will also help you,
I will also uphold you with My righteous right hand."*

- Isaiah 41:10, NASB

VALLEY OF FEARS
-FRIGHTENING PLACES

Our journey through this chapter is taking us to an imaginary that I like to call *the Valley of Fears*. This fictitious place, which houses all the things that could make anybody feel fearful of something or someone. As we scrutinize this feeling, let us look for its causes and effects on the lives of those who experience this emotion.

Rather than analyzing the whole topic in a single chapter, we have divided it into several chapters. Each chapter contains specific information about different aspects of the problems with fears. This scrutiny of fears is aimed to help us grasp a better understanding of the origin and mechanics of fears. Let us get started.

Places That Can Frighten Some People

Typically, people are not afraid of going to places that already occupied by someone or something. The same is true about empty spaces; most people are not intimidated by them either. Nevertheless, some individuals may feel and show signs of fear when going to many different places.

For instance, some individuals are fearful of going to high places (roofs), closed places (elevators), open places (esplanades), and dark places among other locations.

These folks' apprehensiveness is usually linked to the anxiety or discomfort they feel while staying in those places. Once fear kicks in, these people may experience a variety of reactions that could go from a simple chill to a frenetic panic attack.

Imagine that somebody who is afraid of heights has been asked to stand on the roof of a tall building. It is very likely that this person would feel petrified by such request. I am prone to empathize with these types of individuals.

You see, I am not afraid of heights, but I seriously doubt that I would ever be able to stand on the roof top of any skyscraper. I am pretty sure that other people may share this preference with me as well.

However, unlike people who be afraid of altitudes, my apprehension to heights would never prevent me from enjoying the view from any safe outdoor place; yet, if had a choice I would prefer staying indoors, because this is where I tend to feel more comfortable and safer.

Nonetheless, let us forget all about my personals feelings and preferences, and be mindful of people who struggle with fears. Besides, anybody could fall from an altitude and get hurt. Therefore, fearful, or fearless, everybody should always take precautions when standing on high places.

Now let us take a look at this other situation. Some individuals might not be afraid of heights but would not dare going inside places that would make them feel tapped or confined. These folks typically avoid entering to closets, elevators, and small rooms count among the places.

Considering their choices reminds me an occasion in which I went to the hospital for an MRI. The technician performing the test asked me if I was afraid of enclosed spaces. My answer was question negative, but he still gave me a bell, and asked me to call for help if I ever needed it.

Obviously, this technician and other professionals in his field (radiology) are very acquainted with situations in which people have displayed felt enclaustrated while undergoing a radiological screening. Contrary to them are other individuals who would not dare to stay alone inside or around open spaces such as large plazas, big malls, airports, among other spacious places.

These persons' fears and fearful reactions could become a big problem that could deprive them from taking advantage of many modern architectural structures. For instance, nowadays, there are numerous places which contain elevators, which are confined spaces, and esplanades, which are open spaces.

These facilities are not just architectural features, but also important amenities that can save people time and efforts when moving from one floor to another. However, many individuals would rather cancel their commitments than staying in places where they would feel endangered and incapable of escaping from any potential or imaginary "peril" that might be "lurking" around.

The irony of it all is that most places are not dangerous at all. Today's colossal structures contain spaces and amenities that people need and use for the purpose of doing their work, study, shopping, amusement, entertainment, and several other things.

These architectural wonders have been designed to give people many opportunities to do multiple important things a single place. Some of these big buildings are home a great variety of businesses, like universities, hospitals, churches, public halls, galleries, museums, schools, libraries, and other businesses that people visit each day count among these public and commercial entities.

People visit these places not just for the sake of being there, but also because of the many things they can accomplish inside those places can help them carry out their tasks and meet some of their goals. Therefore, simple logic tells us that avoid going to these places could be very disadvantageous for anyone.

Nevertheless, despite these advantages, some people's anxieties and fears may cause them to opt for other alternative ways to go about their affairs and avoid their reality. While pondering upon these things I ask myself this question: should people be afraid of danger?

I do not know how you would answer said question, but I personally think that being afraid of danger is practically impossible. This is because fears are normal reactions that can be experienced by any living creature.

Practical Application

Fear is a feeling that works like an alarm system that warns or alert individuals to take action when danger lurks. This fear alarm tells people that is time to do something, to defend themselves from anyone or anything capable of triggering fearful reaction. From this angle, fear becomes a defense mechanism, which is a good thing to have.

Most fears are born from people's inability to discern the unknown, or what might be brought up by the unknown. Consider this thought, if we were able to know the future in advance, would not we make provisions for the unexpected and be so unafraid of things to come?

Obviously, we do not have this ability. That is why we tend to feel powerless and overtaken by the things that frighten us. This is how fears could turn into enemies.

The fact of the matter is that there is a source or story behind each fear. Finding that source and decoding the stories that may hide behind it, may be the keys to confrontation the problems that turn people into prisoner of their fears.

Danger could be found anywhere. Danger could be found in the high place from which one could fall off and get hurt; in the open space where anybody could get lost or lose something.

Danger can also be found in dark places, where individuals could find creepy creature e.g., crawlers that could harm them, as well as in lonely places, which could be targeted by delinquent and other ill-intentioned criminals. Therefore, fear of danger should not stop anyone from living their life as they should.

Fear of danger could be found in all these places but said fear should never stop anyone from living their life as they should. Fears are reactions, no solutions to the problems that ignite them in the first place.

Despite these facts, people should never let fear take over their lives. Rather, individuals should face reality regardless of their anxieties. This courageous attitude can empower them to move on despite the uncertainties of any evident, apparent or imminent hazardous situation.

Furthermore, there are no gains related to fears; if anything, fears may trigger certain behaviors may translate into social problems. Thus, in the long run, their fears may end up depriving people from trying out new things, making new connections, and having lots of fun with loved ones and acquaintances.

Years ago, I met a woman who was afraid of traveling by airplane. Her fear of flying caused her to miss out on having fun and enjoying quality time with friends and relatives.

Hence, she never went on vacations with her family out of fear of traveling by air or sea. That woman's experience is just one of the many in the list of extreme reactions that people can display when they feel afraid.

Thus, facing their fears will empower individuals to move on with their lives without becoming paralyzed by the thought of going through any real or virtual perilous circumstances. Then, they will be able to go where they need to go and capable of doing the things they must do.

According to some expert behaviorists, fears and anxiety contribute to altering people's emotions to the point of triggering radical behaviors that may cause people to act out.

In that sense, fear becomes an important pathologic element underlying the development of phobias –a fancy name for overgrown or excessive anxiety (please consult appendix for supporting data on this matter).

Appeal

Summing up, fears could rob people of plenty of their ability to reach goals, accomplish tasks, and embracing priceless opportunities to build precious memories with their beloved. Unless they are properly addressed, these unresolved issues could end up isolating people from many things, pleasant and casual.

For these reasons, people must strive to identify the problem that trigger their fears and tackle them. Otherwise, they may go through life feeling afraid of things that may or may not be dangerous or real.

Are you afraid of something? If so, how do you manage your fears? Think about these questions and consider the insights encrypted within the covers of this book. They may lead the way to a fear free life.

Also, keep in mind that by the grace of the Lord, nobody has to face their fears alone anymore. He is with us and is mighty to help us triumph over our fears. God can also give us the victory over anything else that may threaten our mental sanity or the stability of our lives. Do you believe in Him?

"Be still before the Lord and wait patiently for him; do not fret when people succeed in their ways, when they carry out their wicked schemes."

"Refrain from anger and turn from wrath; do not fret --it leads only to evil."

- Psalms 37:7,8, NIV

VALLEY OF FEARS – NATURAL SOURCES

Fears of Animals and Other Creatures

Animals are a very lovable part of nature that many people like to have and bond with. However, on several instances, some animals and insects are the primary sources of people's fears and phobias. Unfortunately, there is not too much that can be done to ameliorate the external factors linked to the sources of this type of fear.

Little creatures are important too!

We share our environment with many living things, including insects and a wide variety of animals. Their mutual interaction with us and our environment is important for the stability of our planet's ecology. Therefore, getting rid of some species (e.g., insects and crawlers) does not seem to be a good option to solve the problem of fears.

Because of their nature, some insects could cause certain individuals to feel threatened or frighten. However, when it comes to these creatures, the best approach is to act safe and being cautious at all times.

Besides, nature can take care of its own. For instance, numerous insects can help cleaning up the environment; but many larger animals eat up these insects, ridding the environment from them. Thus, in the long run, everything balances off.

However, people should always be cautious, because numerous hair-raising insects and crawlers could be poisonous, and in some instances deadly. Moreover, many insects could be vectors for the transmission of several illnesses.

They could also trigger allergic reactions, invade our homes, infest our pantries, and so forth. For these reasons, it is best to put one's fears aside and be on the alert for any winged, hairy, and disgusting insect that could be roaming around our indwelling places.

Some of these creatures could be quite harmless, but one should not take any chances. Therefore, though apparently contradictory, getting rid of nuisances such as ants, cockroaches, creepy crawler, and other types of pests, is not such a bad idea after all.

The issue with animals is a completely different ball game. Numerous animals are domestic and harmless whereas many others could be very dangerous. Certainly, some wild creatures have been tamed by special trainers.

Nevertheless, these trainers are not ordinary people. They are experts whose special skills and abilities enable them to interact with animals safely. Their goal is to do their best job with animals without harming them or being hurt by them.

Hence, animal trainers and caretakers employ their skills and abilities to ensure the protection of animals lovers and other defenseless creatures. The successes of those workers prove that, when wanted and needed, people can still find safe ways to approach wildlife in their own habitats and other surroundings.

Many animals can benefit humans in various ways, For example, in many countries, people use horses, donkeys, mules, camels, and other species as bearers of things needed to make foods and other goods. Hence, it could be said that those animals collaborate with humans in the production of things needed for their own usage and consumption.

Additionally, some animals have been used as the building blocks for other the processing and elaboration of other products. For example, some hats, purses, shoes, and clothing have been made out of the skin or fur of some animals (snakes, crocodiles, bears, among others). Other animals have been used as the primary source of meats that reach the public's hands via supermarkets, restaurants, and other places.

Furthermore, animals can perform roles that can be intertwined with other important and beneficial aspects of human (and animal) living. For instance, many animals could become faithful and loving pets and companions that could help their owners and other people who depend on them, to go about their daily affairs in more efficient ways.

Some of them have been trained to serve their owners as service pets such as guide dogs, law enforcement canines, and comfort pets, among others. These animals can provide companionship and emotional support to their owners.

Some animals can complement the roles of their owner's ears, noses, eyes, hands, feet. Therefore, in several instances, their pets have prevented many catastrophes and save their owner's lives. Therefore, animals are important and special, especially those who are tamed and domesticated.

Despite these things, it is important to keep in mind that animals are inferior beings, whose brains do not process thoughts and ideas in the same manner as the human brains. Their level of reasoning and brain capacities are not as highly elaborated as ours.

Schnapps2012/ Shutterstock

Take zero chances with wildlife!

Often times, animals' instincts could trigger adverse, and even violent reactions that may carry the potential of disrupting the physical and emotional integrity of those who are attacked by them.

For these reasons, people should take precautions when interacting with even including the tamest creature, and they must do this without feeling or showing any fear. Growing up I was told that human fear could be perceived by animals as a potential threat.

Whenever this happens, animals may feel frightened and act defensively, or attack their victims. Hence, smart people should always be cautious when interacting with domestics, domesticated, and wild animals.

Unfortunately, many animal lovers treat some animal species almost in the same way as they would treat another human, and in some cases, perhaps even better. This is a risky behavior that, in the long run, might end up badly.

There have been reports of people who have been attacked by the same creature they have been loving and nurturing all along. If you have ever watched videos or heard stories of people who have been attacked by their pets (snakes, tigers, cats, dogs, etc.), then, you will surely understand the point I am trying to stress here.

Several people have posted on social media some pictures and videos that were intended to amuse the people who watch them. I do not know about other folks, but I find nothing funny about posting a video of a pet which is attacking somebody who was just trying to play with it. If anything, these videos stress the importance of interacting with animals in rational ways that could ensure everyone's safety.

Practical Application

Certainly, there have been many wonderful and magic moments involving relationships between humans and animals. However, there have also been reports of many sad and tragic events involving interactions between animals and humans. Does this mean that I oppose human-animal interactions? Not at all, I just like to think safe.

My take on this matter is a conservative one; we do not need to be afraid of animals, but we should always interrelate with them in cautious ways. Thus, we must love, protect, and respect animals in their environment; but we must also be mindful of who they are, and what they are capable of doing when acting instinctively.

Appeal

The Lord is with us in the spirit, invisible but always by our side. He is powerful to deliver you from any dangerous creature that may want to hurt you. Therefore, I encourage you to trust and worship Him. Sing His praises and say:

"*I will lift up my eyes to the hills, where does my help come from? My help comes from the Lord, the Maker of heaven and earth.*

He will not let your foot slip, He who watches over you will not slumber; indeed, He who watches over Israel will neither slumber, nor sleep.

The Lord watches over you, the Lord is your shade at your right hand; the sun will not harm you by day, or the moon by night.

The Lord will keep you from all harm. He will watch over your life. The Lord will watch over your coming and going both now and forevermore."

(Psalm 121, NIV)

Acts of violence can ruin many lives.

VALLEY OF FEARS – XENOPHOBIA

Fears of Relating with Other People

Many things can be said about people and their relationships each other. People can share special time with each other; they can do things together.

Many people can help solve each other's problems, and work with each other's projects. People are supposed to love and protect each other, but sometimes, they can also hurt, betray, and abandon each other both, voluntarily and involuntarily.

Many people are convicted criminals that have done terrible things; some others are offenders, which had made bad mistakes or done things that have hurt other folks.

On other instances, the behavior of some individuals may raise the red flags of suspicion against them, warning others to be careful. Despite these facts, a person should never be afraid of another human being.

Surely, we must be cautious, thoughtful, and respectful of one another, because respecting each other people's rights is the road to peaceful living. Kindness, honesty, and integrity are very important as well.

Good human-human interactions also require that people learn to apply common sense to their relationships at all times, because associating with some types of people could be potentially dangerous.

Once a person becomes aware that a given individual (or group of people) is dangerous, disrespectful, or dishonest, the next and more appropriate thing to do is avoiding the company of such individual [s]. However, each person must be cautious to avoid hurting other people's feelings or cause them any harm.

Some folks may want to take revenge on others because of something that has been done to them or to somebody they love. However, revenge is another road that can lead to violence and sorrows; therefore, it should be avoided at all cost.

Other individuals may use and abuse drugs or engage in other types of misconduct. They may appear to be very nice. However, some of these "nice" people have done bad or inappropriate things that could be deemed as unlawful.

Avoiding the company of these 'nice folks is the best way to evade sharing their blame for the felonies they have committed. It is always wiser taking the detour at that intersection than engaging in a journey that might end up hurting one's integrity or harming lots of other people.

Some individuals who are mentally handicapped or emotionally unstable, are not fully aware that their actions can turn them into a living menace for themselves and others.

Believe it or not, some gang member and other potentially dangerous individuals might also be unaware that their behaviors are perceived as threats that could jeopardize many lives, including theirs.

Often times, their loved ones and acquaintances of these persons may perceive that something is not quite right with their loved ones. Then, these good-intentioned people realize that something has to be done to help their loved ones.

Many families may have a hard time accepting the implications of the problems affecting their loved ones. This situation may cause these persons to neglect the responsibilities they have towards their loved owns. Consequently, these loved ones might not take all the necessary step to solve those problem, or at least minimize them.

In some instances, loved ones –including spouses, parents, other relatives, and friends, are prone to think that they can change or control the unacceptable or inappropriate behavior of loved ones which have mental, behavioral, or social disturbances. This is a fallacy that could lead to much pain and sorrow.

Their intentions may be noble, but friends and relatives who excuse their loved one's behaviors are not helping at all. By taking the wrong line of action, these individuals may wrongfully or unintentionally block their loved ones' path to solving or preventing some serious problems.

Love should never blind anyone to the reality of seeing things as they are. Thus, people must be opened to realize that people they are trying to "protect" have a problem that must be addressed properly. Some of those individuals need help because they have chosen a path that may lead to a life of crime, which could harm many lives, including theirs.

In several instances, troubled individuals may get away with their felonies. However, people who commit serious felonies belong in a prison cell until they learn to become productive members of society. However, if those felonies have any link to a mental or emotional disturbance, folks should undergo a comprehensive mental evaluation and proceed accordingly.

Doctors and other behaviorists can help mentally challenged persons to find solutions for their problems. Every day, we hear about some horror story of some bad thing that a mentally-challenged individual have done to somebody These types of incidents call for expert help and close supervision of the individuals implied in those happenings.

Loved ones and acquaintances may do their best to try to avoid these types of occurrences. However, they cannot handle problems that fall beyond the scope of their competency. For this reason, mentally-challenged individuals need to be treated by licensed mental health professional.

These experts are qualified to help their clients find better ways to deal with their health issues. The aggressive therapies they provide to their clients can help ensure more positive outcomes for their mental conditions. Therefore, it is always best to let doctors, behaviorists, law enforcement, and other authority figures, to handle certain people and certain situations.

Cards on the table: Being afraid of socially, emotionally, or mentally challenged folks is not the best thing to do. Contrarily, becoming more aware of these people's conditions, and trying to avoid disturbing them would be a much better approach.

Many individuals with certain mental or emotional conditions are practically harmless when they are not being disturbed by others, whereas other persons could be very dangerous even without provocation. They could hurt themselves and others regardless of having been challenged by others or not.

On some instances, these people's feelings and reactions are directly linked to the pathophysiology of the disease that have taken the hold of their minds. Example, some people with dementia might feel frighten and attack the people who are trying to help them.

Considering all these things, it is easier to understand why some people could feel apprehensive around individuals who have mental and social impairments. However, rather of being fearful, people should be cautious around mentally impaired individuals.

Although impaired, these folks are also humans who have needs like everybody else. Therefore, persons must take all the necessary precautions before helping them out with things like, giving them water, food, clothing, blankets, etc.

Practical Application

In addition to taking all the appropriate measures to deal with troubled individuals and the situation that may arise from their erratic behaviors.

Also, it is essential to give God a chance to take control over our life's situations. He is the ultimate Helper, and as Paul the apostle once said: "*What then shall we say to these things? If God is for us, who is against us?* (Romans 8:31, NASB).

God can help people find solutions for their problems. He can comfort for their souls and help them endure the test of their circumstances. Faith-driven individuals can be renewed their strengths by way of trusting in the Lord's promises. Here is a precious promise that has helped many people cope with some problems involving their loved ones:

"*But this is what the Lord says: 'Yes, captives will be taken from warriors, and plunder retrieved from the fierce; I will contend with those who contend with you and your children I will save'*" (Isaiah 49: 25, NIV).

Therefore, abiding in the confidence that rises from God's promises can help faith-driven individuals to moving forward regardless of their circumstances. Surely, there are times in which despite believing in God's promises and finding inner strengths in them, troubling situations continue to pile up and threaten to smother these believers.

Their adversities might give believers multiple reasons to be fearful or distrust in the power of God's Word. What is there to do then? Well, letting fear and distress take the hold of one's life will never be a good option. Rather, people of faith should refuse to give in to their distresses and remain willing to submit their affairs and feelings unto the Lord (Psalms 34:7).

Appeal

God answers the prayers of His children and can help them find their way out of their problems. He can take care of everything that troubles their minds. Hence, if you ever encounter anyone whose erratic behavior causes you to quiver in fear, do not be afraid. Remember that the Lord is always with you.

God can protect and rescue you from anybody, trouble, or situation. Many troublesome things happen in the world each day; but if you fear and worry about the actions of evildoers, I want you to encourage you to trust in God. Know that He set a date and time to deal with evil, for it is written:

"*The transgressors shall be destroyed together; the end of the wicked shall be cut off. But the salvation of the righteous is of the Lord; He is their strength in the time of trouble*" (Psalms 37:38, 39, KJV).

These verses can help us infer that sometimes it may appear as if the Lord was taking a long time to fulfill His promise. However, they also contain a promise of salvation, which should encourage His faithful believers to hold steadfast to their convictions because in His time, the Lord will do what must be done.

---

*"I sought the Lord, and He heard me,
And delivered me from all my fears."*

- Psalm 34:4, NKJV

VALLEY OF FEARS – EMOTIONAL SOURCES

Fear of Experiencing Emotions

Our feelings are key to the quality of our lives. Hence, living in fear can hold us back and prevent us to reach our most cherished goals. Fear of failure, fear of doing something wrong, fear of losing something or someone, fear of loving, fear of living, fear of dying, fear of anger, and believe it or not, even fear of being happy, all of these and many others are common feelings that people experience every day and everywhere.

However, since fears can be like a stumbling rock blocking our paths to successful living. Therefore, we must despise negative feelings like distresses and fears, and harbor positive feelings like faith, hope, love, and joy. This initiative will help us be happier and better able to reach our goals.

Giving in to their fears could render folks to feel incapable of doing anything right. Then, like cowards, these persons are likely to remain paralyzed by a feeling that could prevent them from reaching the upmost of their potential.

Fear of Living

Believe it or not, life itself could become a source of fear. How could this be? Allow me to answer this rhetorical question with the assistance of the following examples.

First, let us say that you are aware of something that could harm you or somebody else. If so, you would probably fear for your life or the life of this other person; wouldn't you? Consequently, this type of fear may cause you to remain silent.

Finding out that you are very ill or that you need to undergo an urgent major surgical procedure would probably cause you to fear for your life as well.

People who live in perilous places know about being afraid. They know what is like being surrounded by felons and delinquents. They know what happens whenever stray bullets fly aimlessly around their homes.

These people also know what is like realizing that people disappear from the area without leaving any traces, and no one would know a thing about them. I firmly believe that people who live under those circumstances would feel afraid of living.

These examples have been taking straight out of everyday life. We hear similar accounts on the newscasts, read about them in the newspapers, and watch their images on television and social media outlets.

Each one of those accounts describes many things that could happen to the living. Dead people do not have to worry about what may happen to them or to their loved ones. Therefore, those who are alive are the ones who can actually react to these types of news.

Fortunately, there is more to life than being afraid of living. Look at the roses. They have thorns that can hurt, but people disregard their spikes and focus on appreciating their awesome aromas and beautiful appearance.

Similarly, life is filled with ups and downs, good things, and bad things. Thus, people who would like to live life to the fullest must learn to take in the good things and turn them into even greater things.

Then again, what should be done with the bad things that strip happiness out of one's life? The best thing to do would be avoid engaging in any troublesome things and situations. This approach would be utopic but is not always feasible. Hence, we all need to learn to juggle our situations in ways that can make it possible for us to turn bad things into good things.

Certainly, life could give us numerous reasons to be afraid, but we should never give in to any of those reasons. Instead, we should always look at the brighter side of things and try finding newer and better reasons to live by each day.

Life is a gift from God. He can help us deal with all of our situations –good ones and bad ones. Hence, let us live life boldly and make the most of the days that the Creator has given us on this Earth! Let us confidently proclaim:

"*When I am afraid, I will trust in you. In God, whose word I praise, in God I trust; I will not be afraid*" (Psalm 56:3, 4, NIV).

Fear of Dying

We have previously stated that individuals who are very sick and those who live in hostile or "risky" neighborhoods are likely to fear for their lives. However, what can be said about people who live and good areas? Well, they too may have their own encounters with death. Consider the following circumstances.

People who have been involved in serious accidents,

Individuals who have had close encounters with wild animals,

Persons who have been assaulted by criminals and other malefactors,

Folks who have been caught in the path of major storms,

And people who live near war zones,

All these individuals have the same thing in common: at some point in their lives, they all have feared for their lives. They all have had close encounters with death and have barely escaped alive from its terrifying grip.

Certainly, fear of dying is not a fable, is a crude part of the circle of life, which we all have to face sooner or later. Nevertheless, we all prefer the "later" rather than the "sooner."

Henceforth, if we want to improve the quality of our lives, we must learn to set ourselves free from all types of fears, including fear of dying. Trust in God and His promises can help individuals achieve this goal. The Holy Scriptures say:

"For you did not receive a spirit that makes you a slave again to fear, but you received the Spirit of sonship. And by him we cry 'Abba, Father" (Romans 8:15, NIV).

This means that, once we accept the Lord in our lives, we are automatically adopted into the heavenly family as God's children. Therefore, no chain should be strong enough to tie us up.

Folks who abide in the Lord can find freedom from fear and from anything else that might threaten our chances of enjoying life to the fullest. Let us allow Him to lead our ways, and He will make our days brighter, better, and more enjoyable.

Practical Application

Everybody yearns to live happily and fear free, including individuals who struggle with feelings of sadness and despair. They too want to be joyful, prosperous, and fruitful.

Therefore, folks must be reluctant to worry excessively about their fears and feelings. They must not allow themselves to become distracted with thoughts of what has happened or will happen. Success-driven individuals should wear the armor of courage, dare to take risks, and give themselves second chances to live better lives .

These are secrets are like weapons to fight distresses, discouragements, and fears that can empower individuals to fight their battles and win many victories. With God's help, more than a statement this could be a norm to live by (Philippians 4:13).

Therefore, let us be mindful of God's promises; they can give us confidence to move on with our lives. The Word of God tells us:

"Have no fear of sudden disaster or of the ruin that overtakes the wicked, for the Lord will be your confidence and will keep your foot from being snared" (Proverbs 3:25, 26, NIV). *"Be strong and courageous. Do not be terrified; do not be discouraged, for the Lord your God will be with you wherever you go"* (Joshua 1:9, NIV).

VALLEY OF FEARS – EMOTIONAL SOURCES

Appeal

There are many terrifying dangers and perils that could threaten our lives each day and anywhere; but the Lord has promised to protect us all the days of our lives. Thus, let us trust in Him. Then, when the time of our departure comes by, we will fear death no longer because the Lord will be with us and give us confidence to sleep in peace.

God has assured us that even if we die before the Second Advent of His Son, He will rise us up in the last day (John 6:40). Paul the apostle was persuaded of this fact and advised the early Christians to comfort one another with these words (1Thessalonians 4:16-18).

Therefore, be cheerful despite the troubles and always remember that the Lord is with you. He can cast your fears away (1Peter 5:7) and help you live life in abundance(John 10:10). Do you believe this?

Fear Not! God is with you.

*"Blessed be the Lord, my rock,
who trains my hands for war,
and my fingers for battle."*

- Psalms 144, ESV

THE FEAR FACTOR

Feeling afraid or apprehensive on account of the things that has happened or could happen to us is almost unavoidable. In fact, practically everybody has been acquainted with this feeling sometime and somewhere. Who can deny this reality? Fear is everywhere. Therefore, this feeling must be addressed properly and timely (as soon as possible).

Nevertheless, facing one's fears is not the same as engaging in risky behaviors such as climbing the highest mountain, performing acrobatics on the back of a motorcycle, jumping off out of a car that is already in motion, or walking on ropes over a cliff. Being able to do these things does not mean that a person is brave. It means that this person has successfully engaged in some type of risky behavior.

These dexterities are typically performed by free-spirited people who want to try out something new in life. They may want to put on a show (e.g., acrobatics), or to dare to do something rare or amazing just for the fun of it, or just to prove a point. Therefore, doing these things does not mean that a person is fearless; it means that the person performing these things is bold and daring.

Facing one's fears implies becoming acquaintance with the things, sources, and triggers of one's fears and making good choices that may empower us to live on despite any dreadful circumstances.

Therefore, people must fight their fears to break free from them. The process of fighting and overcoming one's fears can involve making some adjustments in one's life. However, these adjustments should not involve decisions that may restrain or jeopardize a person's life.

Contrarily, resisting one's fears and refusing to make major life style modifications that may restrict one's living are the epitome of being brave and achieving freedom from fears.

Persons might find themselves entangled in the midst of dangerous situations, which might call for them to physically defending themselves from danger. Then again, what would happen to those folks if they let their fears take a hold over their lives? Wouldn't this situation render these fearful individuals incapable of doing the right thing at the right time? The most likely the answer to this question is yes.

Not being able to react properly in the midst of danger could be disastrous. Rather than defending themselves, these folks would let ear take over and will likely lose rational control over their movements, thoughts, and decisions. Under those circumstances, the people who are afraid could unintentionally endanger their own wellbeing, or inadvertently hurt some other unsuspected individuals.

This reminds me the story of a man who heard a noise in the middle of the night. Thinking that there was a thief in the house, the man fired his gun towards the place where he had previously heard the noise.

The man turned the lights on and to his surprise and despair, there was no thief in the house. The man lying lifeless on the floor was none other than his own son, who had just returned from a night of fun with his friends.

Fear caused that father to point and shoot his gun; and because of fear, and the guilt of losing his son in such tragic way will likely haunt him for the rest of his life.

There are many other incidents like this one. All of them are examples of things that have happened to people who have left fears take over their lives; then, their uncertain circumstances have turned into catastrophic incidents.

Many of these occurrences have become headlines news. Therefore, it is likely that as you read these lines through, you may also be recalling some of these occurrences. It is also possible that you have already witnessed or at least heard talks concerning similar occurrences.

Practical Application

People can do many odd and even irrational things when they are afraid. However, their actions and reactions might be at the root of their problems but are not the problem per se. In other words, the problem with fears does not resides on feeling afraid, but on not knowing how to face one's fears; that is the real problem.

Fears and phobias can imprison people and disrupt the quality their lives. Fears can also submerge its victims into a world of panic, which may have detrimental effects on their physical and emotional health.

Fear can rob individuals of their peace of minds and disrupt the relationships of people who have been imprisoned by it. Fortunately, the Lord can empower individuals to build stronger and longer lasting relationships with others.

Appeal

Fears can lower people's quality of life. Therefore, persons must face their fears, tackle them, and wipe them away if possible. Thankfully, there are many solutions available to people who want to leave a fear free life. One of them is casting one's fears at the feet of the Lord.

God is the fear killer and the One who cares for us (1Peter 5:7). Trust in this Mighty warrior can turn folks into happier and more confident persons. Hence, I encourage you to abide in the comfort of this thoughts and find freedom from distress and fears through faith in God.

*"Even youths grow tired and weary,
and young men stumble and fall;
but those who hope in the Lord
will renew their strength."*

*"They will soar on wings like eagles;
they will run and not grow weary,
they will walk and not be faint."*

- Isaiah 40:30, 31, NIV

HOW TO LIVE A FEARLESS LIFE

"Living in fear" does not necessarily means that individuals cannot free themselves from the bondage of fears. Although challenging, persons can find freedom from fears by way of fighting back against this feeling; but how can they do it? What kind of things can people do to live a fear free life?

Try to answer those questions as we over the following set of practical suggestions to deal with the problem of fears. Let us get started.

Tips and Hints for a Fear Free Life.

---

a.) Seek for Help

Fears are involuntary responses to someone or something that is perceived as threatening. In other words, people do not tell themselves or plan to be afraid. They just cannot help becoming afraid of the things that trigger this feeling in the first place.

When people get afraid, their bodies release several adverse responses that cause individuals to feel bad. These bodily responses range from becoming lightheaded, to feeling short of breath and racing or pounding heart beats, also known as tachycardia. Some individuals may also present symptoms of abdominal cramping, weakness, headaches, and other physical responses.

Anybody who has ever felt panic or fear is well acquainted with these corporal responses. The bigger their fears, the stronger the symptomatic responses to their situations. For instance, whenever a person, or another vehicle comes out of nowhere and cut in front of me, I am forced to apply the brakes to prevent an accident, but then I get a terrible headache, nauseas, lightheadedness, tachycardia.

This and other biological reactions are the channels through which the human body warns us that something is not quite right; these warning signs usually go away as fast as they appear.

However, if the physical manifestations of fear do not go away soon, the individuals who experience them will likely have several difficulties coping with their issues. Hence, folks must be able to work out some positive ways to face their problems. Otherwise, they would need to seek for professional from expert behaviorists that may help them overcome their problems.

b.) *Identify Your Human Network of Support*

In addition to counseling, therapies, and biological treatments, the warm support of loved ones and acquaintances can help individuals combat their problems. On some instances, human support could be as important as taking conventional prescription drugs.

A popular adage says: "it takes two to tango." This statement is a strong pillar of truth. Think about this, getting professional help can help individuals to manage their problems. However, in matters of behavioral health, this expert help alone might not be enough to make people's fears go away for good.

Hence, professional help works alongside with the loving support of kind friends and loved ones. Together, these approaches can make a sizable difference in the lives of individuals who struggle to overcome negative emotions like fears.

Relatives, friends, acquaintances, and other kinds of caring people may couch fearful persons and help them achieve their wellness goals. In that sense, people's loved ones become a network of support, which fosters psychological help and medical treatment.

This, human support could be one of the best ways to help persons striving to overcome fears, phobias, and panic attacks, and find solutions for the problems that trigger these feelings. Thus, human support can help change things for the better; as one hand is holding the other, people come to realize that they have someone in which they can count on.

In addition, the kindness, compassion, and understanding support of their love ones can encourage the fearful person to face their fears more assertively. Perhaps this is why support groups have become such a popular and positive alternative to help individuals overcome many negative emotions.

Friends and relatives are people's strongest network of support

c.) Be Determined

Nobody can undermine the role that behaviorist and good-hearted individuals play in helping people fight their fears. People who struggle with fears and other negative emotions need to apply their personal efforts to fight their problems.

Hence, their determination to fight their battles becomes essential to help them overcome the problems these individuals are trying to overcome. Similarly, the willingness to move forward in life goes hand-in-hand with people's determination to attain freedom from fears.

Therefore, no treatment can substitute the will power of a person who is willing to free themselves from the problems that hurdle them down. Those who use all the resources available to them are more likely to succeed in their efforts to overcome the situations that ignite their fears.

d.) Move Forward in Faith

In addition to getting professional help, having a strong human support of loved ones to help out, and the will power to overcome the hurdles, individuals must also have open mindedness. All these things work together to help persons cope and conquer their fears.

Having an open mind can help individuals "think outside the box" and consider alternative solutions for their problems. Believe it or not, exploring spiritual approaches is also another good option to fight fears. One spiritual approach that could help individuals overcome their negative emotions is faith.

Faith is believing with wholeheartedness. Faith is the substance of things we hope for, and the demonstration of the unseen (Hebrews 11:1). Therefore, faith is an option that can help individuals to succeed on their when everything else have failed.

Faith is upholding the assurance of having a compassionate Healer that can rid everyone from fears and emotional sufferance. This Healer is none other than the Creator, the One who knows us best inside and out, the fear killer, the Almighty God.

Practical Application

Fears can make people become unhappy and somber and cause them to throw "shadows" onto other people's paths intentionally or inadvertently. This is how fears can also interfere with people's abilities to brighten the lives of other people in their lives.

Fears can give birth to many negative outcomes and ruin people's lives on many different levels. Hence, fears should not have a permanent place in the life of nobody.

Fortunately, people who trust Him with all their situations will be able to hope for the best and sing praises to the Lord. By faith folks can experience God's power to cast away all fears and set people free from any other sort of bondage. He can replace fears with hope, confidence, and praise.

Appeal

Are you struggling with fears that are making negative impressions in your life? What steps have you taken towards solving the problems or situations that trigger your fears? Who is helping you tackle and overcome this feeling?

Consider these questions and answer them with honesty. Also, continue to work on finding solutions to eradicate your fears and remember that God is always by your side. He can help you find solutions for your problems and replace your fears with confident hopes for better thing to come.

"I have found David, my servant; with my holy oil I have anointed him."

- Psalms 89:20, ESV

THE KING WHO OVERCAME HIS FEARS THROUGH FAITH

This chapter contain more information on this topic of overcoming fears through faith. We will talk about David, a man who struggled with several negative emotions that caused him to feel emotionally hurt. He learned to overcome conquer the situations that brought fears and afflictions into his life. Let us now go over a fragment of his story.

David was an ancient king who was very acquainted with the problem of fear. He fought and won many battles; yet he struggled to overcome numerous situations that brought fears into his life. As he went through his situations, this ruler learned to trust in God, and in time, he found deliverance from his fears.

One day, while meditating in the goodness and greatness of his Rescuer, David wrote a new song of hope and praise. It was a song of confidence in God, the shelter of his life. Here is a fragment of that song:

He who dwells in the shelter of the Most High will abide in the shadow of the Almighty. I will say to the Lord, 'My refuge and my fortress, My God in whom I trust'.

For it is He who delivers you from the snare of the trapper and from the deadly pestilence. He will cover you with His pinions and under His wings you may seek refuge; His faithfulness is a shield and bulwark.

You will not be afraid of the terror by night, or of the arrow that flies by day; or of the pestilence that stalks in darkness, or of the destruction that lays waste at noon. A thousand may fall at your side, and ten thousand in your right hand. But it shall not approach you.

You will only look on with your eyes and see the recompense of the wicked. For you have made the Lord, my refuge, even the Most High, your dwelling place, no evil will befall you, nor will any plague come near your tent.

For He will give His angels charge concerning you to guard you in all your ways. They will bear you up in their hands that you do not strike your foot against a stone. You will tread upon the lion and the cobra, the young lion, and the serpent you will trample down.

Because he has loved Me, therefore, I will deliver him; I will set him on high, because he has known my name. He will call upon Me, and I will answer him. I will be with him in trouble, I will rescue him and honor him with a long life I will satisfy him and let him see my salvation (Psalms 91, NASB).

This wonderful Psalm has been a source of comfort for individuals undergoing difficulties throughout the centuries. It talks about a Mighty deliverer who is always ready to protect the children of His creation. He sees them through their conflicts and grants their petitions by the power of His grace.

The Bible tells us about many people who found shelter under the wings of the Almighty One. King David was one of them. In moments of distress and fear, this king called upon the Lord, and God delivered him from all his torments.

Each time the Lord came through for him, King David felt such happiness that he praised the Lord with melodious accords. One of these melodious carols Davide made this affirmation: *"I sought the Lord and He delivered me from all my fears"* (Psalm 34:4, NASB).

Like in David's days, today, there are millions of people whose lives are also tied up with the chains of fear. The impact of this negative feeling in their lives have caused numerous persons to experience physical discomfort, despair, and uncertainties.

Rather than acknowledging their problems and reach out to those who can help them out, some persons who struggle with fears opt for ignoring or pampering their feelings. Unless they change their minds, these individuals will not be able to find relief for their minds.

Other folks seek for solutions to their problems by way of relying in the expert therapeutic treatments and advise of professional behaviorists and mental healthcare workers.

The mighty grace of God, which always watches over His children can also help people get relieve from their anxieties and improve their quality of life. People who take advantage of these resources can find freedom from their distresses and fears like David did.

Practical Application

Fear could interfere with our relationships, but it should not destroy them. It can hold people emotionally captive and take away their chances of being happy.

Fears may shake us, but it should not paralyze us. Fears may hurt us, but it should not kill us. Therefore, fearful individuals should never let fears take control over their minds or take away their appetite, sleep, or will to live.

Fear could hold us prisoners of ourselves and our problems. Thereby, fear is our enemy, and what should be done with enemies? They should be targeted, fought, and conquered. The same should be done with fears: Face them, fight them, and conquer them.

This is not an easy task, but with God's help all things are possible (Philippians 4:13). Many folks strive to rid themselves from their fears, but God is always there, ready, willing, and able to help people solve their problems.

Appeal

The grace of God can transform your life. He can break the chains of fears that bind your soul. Then, like David's your joyful heart will also sing this song:

I sought the Lord, and He answered me, and delivered me from all my fears. They looked to Him and were radiant, and their faces will never be ashamed. This poor man cried, and the Lord heard him and saved him out of all his troubles.

The angel of the Lord encamps around those who fear Him and rescues them. O taste and see that the Lord is good; how blessed is the man who takes refuge in Him! (Psalm 34: 4-8, NASB).

Therefore, do not be afraid to cast your fears and all your situations at the feet of the Lord. He is the best antidote against anxiety and fears and the One who can make you whole. Do you have that confidence in you?

LEARNING TO WALK ON WATER

Fear is not a new element in this planet. Millions of people have struggled with this emotion throughout the centuries, and many of them found deliverance from this foe through faith. We have already mentioned the experience of David, the ancient king who struggled to overthrow their fears. Now, we are going to talk about Peter's experience.

Peter was one of Jesus' disciples. From the outside, he was apparently unbreakable; but this man was in desperate need of experiencing God's grace and power to overcome fears. He was very outrageous throughout all the seasons in his life. This impetuous disciple thought of himself as a brave man, but he was oblivious of his own fallibilities.

Like many other persons before and after him, Peter was vulnerable to uncertainties and fears. Hence, his character needed to undergo a complete makeover. The day came when, despite his negative traits and behavioral tendencies, Peter came face to face with a dreadful reality that changed his perception of fear radically.

Up until that moment, the intrepid apostle had always seemed to know what do about everything. He never thought about it, but Peter was about to get caught up by fear in a very public, embarrassing, and unavoidable way.

The day it happened, Peter boarded the boat with the rest of Jesus' disciples. Jesus had told them to go ahead without Him, and that He would meet them on the other side of the shore. The men listened and obeyed. As they sailed away, the peaceful a dark and gloomy coat that covered their peaceful evening and turned into a terrifying night that they would never forget.

The wind was whistling, and the waves were raging; the disciples were afraid. Suddenly, they saw a figure in the distance. It looked as if someone were walking on the water; but how could that be? They could not understand this mysterious occurrence.

Something incredible was happening and their eyes could not believe what they were seeing. You see, everyone knows that it is impossible for the living to walk on water without sinking. However, these disciples were seemingly seeing otherwise. Panic took the hold of their minds as the terrified men exclaimed: "it must be a ghost!"

Meanwhile, Jesus, continued to walk towards the boat. He is capable of discerning everybody's thoughts and feelings; hence, He was well aware of the disciples' fears. He knows about our fears too. The "phantom" was fast approaching them, and the terrorized crew did not know what to do. Then, with sweet accent, Jesus told the frighten men: "Fear not. It is I."

Immediately after that, Peter worked out the boldness to say: "Master, if it is you, command that I walk over the waters." Jesus did not have to prove Himself to His disciples. However, He knew that this disciple (Peter) needed to learn a lesson on trust. He needed to get out of the boat and walk with Jesus on water. Therefore, Jesus said: "Come" and Peter went by at Jesus' command.

The incredulous disciple started walking on the water just like Jesus was. He was not sinking! What a sight should that have been for the other disciples! What an amazing feeling for Peter!

I imagine on that moment, Peter must have felt like a supernatural creature. I also imagine that the excitement of the moment might have caused Peter to forget that his current experience was all about the Master's doing. Peter has nothing to do with his ability to defy gravity while walking on water, but Jesus did. He has power over nature, and Peter was about to find that out.

Peter was very elated with what was happening to him. But perhaps he trusted too much in his own humanity. Maybe he started to feel superior to the others, or perchance he lost sight of the target while wandering how in the world was it possible that he could walk on water.

We might never know all the details of that memorable moment, or what thoughts rushed through Peter's mind that night. Nevertheless, we know that in his elation, Peter was too busy to look upon Jesus anymore. He lost sight of his beloved Master and swiftly found himself sinking in the water.

Then, he reacted with real panic and cried out: "Lord, save me for I perish!" Briskly, and before Peter had time to realize what was about to happen, Jesus' hand held his own and pulling him out of the watery grave. Then both, the disciple and his Master continued walking on water.

A huge silence overwhelmed Peter as he walked with Jesus towards the small boat that would take them to the other shore. This time around, Peter was quiet and silenced by the humbling lesson he had just been taught.

Peter, the one who was never quiet; the one who was always ready to utter his opinion, was now silent. How was that possible? The answer is simple: there was nothing to talk about. Peter had seen the face of fear and felt its chilling grip touching his incredulous heart; but he also experienced the saving power of his beloved Master.

As unbelievable as it may seem, this is a true story, whose account is found in Matthew chapter 14, verses 23-33. Each time I read it, I get transported to that boat and become one with the story. Then and there, it is easier for me to realize how Peter learned to cast his fears on his Lord. His experienced taught Peter that only Jesus was perfectly able to make his fears disappear once and for all.

From that day on, Peter had a change of heart. Several years later, while exhorting his flock, Peter, the apostle encouraged his church with this wise advice: "*Casting all your anxiety on Him, because He cares for you*" (1Peter 5:7, NASB).

Practical Application

Peter's experience is the best illustration I can find to tell you that faith in God is the best remedy to end the problem of fear. Only He can strengthen our spirits and give us hope for better outcomes.

Today, we too can take advantage of Peter's advice, make it our own, and experience freedom from fears as this apostle did. People who believe and trust in God can understand this concept very well. This wonderful privilege is also extended to anybody who is eager and willing to learn the secret of remaining still while depending on the Lord.

In order to attain freedom from fears through faith, people must deposit total trust in God and give Him the opportunity to become the ruler of their lives. He knows everything that troubles our lives, and kindly tells us: "*I am the Lord your God who upholds your right hand, who says to you, do not fear, I will help you*" (Isaiah 41:10, NASB).

Certainly, the life and experiences of many ancient heroes of faith can help us understand that faith in the Lord brings hope. When combined, these spiritual attributes can help individuals find freedom from fears. Faith and hope are important tools in the hands of believers who want to experience the power and the blessing of living a fearless life.

Setting His children free from the bondage of fears is God's will for humanity. Jesus encouraged His disciples with these blessed words of hope: "*So, if the Son makes you free, you will be free indeed*" (John 8:36, NASB). If we believe in Him, we too will be free indeed.

Appeal

I firmly believe that there is no better feeling than the assurance of abiding under the shadow of God Almighty. In Him, you, I, anybody, and everybody can enjoy the freedom of living fearlessly in an uncertain world.

Thus, if you have not experienced His joy in your life, I invite you to consider the words you are reading and give yourself the chance to put them to the test. Wouldn't you like to experience such wonderful blessing in your life?

If you give the Lord a special place in your life, He will cause your heart to overflow with joy each time you meditate in His promises. So, do not postpone your decision for much longer. Accept this invitation and live a fearless life in Jesus Christ and embrace His promises.

Also, remember that you are not alone in the midst of your situations. The Lord is with you. He can deliver you from all your fears.

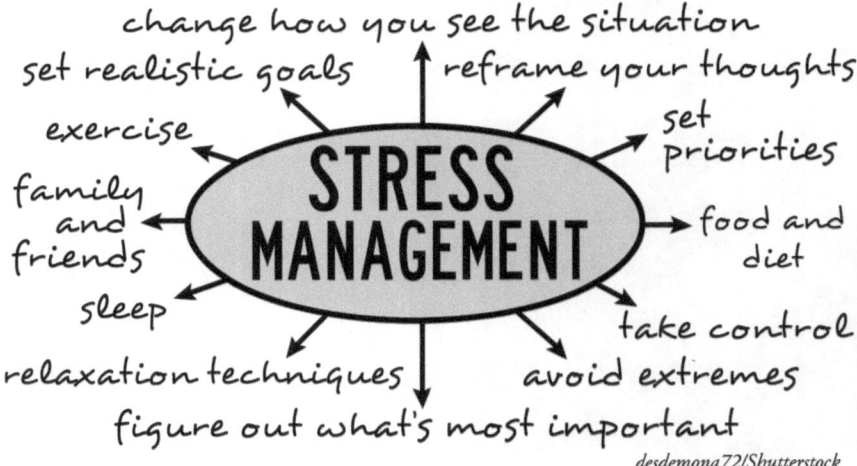

The Lord can give you the wisdom you need to face your challenges and overcome them.

NEGATIVE WAYS TO COPE WITH ADVERSITIES AND FEARS

Can you think of a time in which you were so overtaken by your problems, that amidst your confusion, you lost track of what you should have done? Do not worry. You are neither the first nor the last person who has ever gone through such experience.

Problems are not exclusive properties of any particular individual, as everybody has troubles and trials of their own. However, the ways in which people approach their difficulties can determine the quality of their lives. Therefore, I dare to ask, how do you cope with adversity? What do you do whenever you are dazed by troubles and difficulties?

I cannot answer these questions for you at this time; however, we could try answering these questions together. To that end, let us go over of the things that other people have done when dealing with big problems.

Several years ago, when I was still very young, a terrible financial crisis had devastating consequences for many people in my native Santo Domingo. One after another, several financial institutions started sinking into troubles and filing for bankruptcy.

People were pressuring the bankers for their moneys, as their financial world was crumbling down. I was still very young when these things happened, and truth be told, I was not very interested in watching depressing newscasts either. Therefore, I do not recall all the details of that financial meltdown.

However, I do remember the pandemonium among the people who lost their savings as the result of the market crash. It was the talk of the days. The lives of many rich people were torn apart. There were arguments and divorces everywhere.

Many bankers and investors were badly hurt by this situation. This was one of the saddest and most notorious events that happen back then. After losing a large portion of their assets, and receiving pressure from different angles, these individuals and felt impotent to deal with their problems.

Many of these people died by suicide, Hence, out of all the things that went wrong back in those days, these fatal events were the ones that left the deepest impression in my young mind.

This account serves to illustrate what has happened to some people who have succumbed under the pressure of their difficulties. Although drastic, this is also a very realistic example.

Similar occurrences have also taken place almost everywhere around the world, including numerous rich countries like the United States of America.

When dealing with serious health, financial and personal, social, and other types of situations, many individuals have opted for ending their lives by way of committing suicide. Their decisions have been driven by feelings of distress, despair, and impotence, which rendered them incapable of handling their situations in appropriate and efficient ways.

There have also been some instances in which troubled people have tried to manage their circumstances by way of resorting to drastic and sometimes, questionable measures. Their choices have yielded terrible results that in some instances have caused tons of pain and suffering to many other individuals.

NEGATIVE WAYS TO COPE WITH ADVERSITIES AND FEARS

a.) Overreacting to the Problems

Other folks have blown off in the heat of violent emotional outbursts or gave in to a life of crimes and felonies. Some of them have been abusive to other people, stole other people's property, and even committed murders and murder-suicides.

Then one must ask, why do people do this sort of things? Who can find the right answer for this rhetoric? Every one's mind is a realm of its own. Hence, one can only speculate that perhaps, at some point in time, people become so overwhelmed by their issues and make unwise decisions. Somewhere along the line, these types of folks lost all sense of right or wrong and ended up by choosing wrong instead of the right solution for their problems.

All of these situations have a single pattern in common: the people involved have gone through terrible circumstances, which caused them to do regrettable things. The pressure of their stressors made these folks vulnerable collapse under the pressures of their adversities.

The fact of the matter is that adversity is always standing before us. Therefore, we all should learn to weight the importance of the things that bother us, and then, consider coping mechanisms to deal with those situations.

Now, let us go back to the questions that originated these arguments: How do you cope with your problems? How do you deal with adverse situations? Think of your answers, as we go through the next set of insights.

While undergoing difficulties, people may cope with their situations in positives or negative ways. Their choices may or may not help folks stay afloat in the midst of their adversities. Some approaches are useless to solve any problem, whereas some others may constitute wonderful tools to deal with stressful circumstances.

Assuming that you got the point of this rhetoric, I now dare to ask you to think about a recent incident that may fit any of the previously mentioned profiles. This mental exercise should not take you more than a few seconds.

However, do not worry if you were unable to connect this rhetoric with a current incident. I am convinced that considering the current state of affairs, it might not be long before you hear of some other drastic or tragic thing involving folks who have been struggling with some terrible situations.

These types of occurrences usually happen to people who lose their capacity of thinking things through while undergoing difficulties. Then, they snap out and make bad decisions or commit serious mistakes, which they may regret later in life.

b.) Falling Apart

While struggling with adversities, many people are more vulnerable to feel sad, confused, and anxious. These feelings could lead to anger, irritability, and withdrawal, among others negative sentiments. These feelings can also make people become more susceptible to falling apart or caving under the pressure of the same things that disturb them.

Their attitudes and reactions could predispose some folks to become easy target of the hostility, criticism, or misunderstanding of others other individuals.

The situations affecting these folks could be critical or desperate and may cause them to get stressed-out over their problems. However, the people who criticize them would likely refuse to understand the nature of the feelings and circumstances standing behind the inappropriate reactions of the people who are in trouble.

This is a very delicate scenario because, some persons cannot avoid feeling angry, irritable, sad, or pessimistic while undergoing difficulties. Therefore, these individuals could easily cave under pressure of their unwanted circumstances.

Instead of hostility and criticism, these folks deserve to be treated with patience and respect. They may also need plenty of help and support from others.

They may also have to bear the added burden of facing the murmuring, mockery, and judgmental opinion of other thoughtless people who learned about.

c.) Behavioral Outbursts

Added to their anxieties and difficulties, many individuals, may not know how to properly manage their emotions while undergoing stress. Then, they may snap out on somebody and later on face the consequences for their actions.

Thoughtful individuals are usually more empathetic of weary folks and their situations. Instead of reprimanding and condemning others, caring people are more likely to view people's feelings and patterns of behaviors that would occur in response to adversity.

These natural responses may or may not be the most desirable; but then again, nobody is perfect. At some point in life, everybody is likely to go through some type of drastic situation. However, each human response or reaction to adversity is likely to be faulty because human nature is fallible and subjected to imperfections.

These are facts of life. In the perfect world, there would be no faults or problems; yet, since we live in an imperfect world, we constantly come in contact with troubles and difficulties that could shake us up mercilessly. Sooner or later, everyone has to deal with the unthinkable.

Even the kindest and most humanists, moralists, or religious individual can make terrible mistakes, or get involved in serious scandalous situations. Therefore, people have no right to judge anyone for handling problems differently than what they may consider to be the right way to get things done.

For this reason, it is important that folks educate themselves with information that prepares them beforehand to better handle hardships and difficulties when they finally arrive. Also, it is important to acknowledge that either individually or collectively, people tend to go about their situations in their own unique ways.

Some folks have the tendency to make bad choices; others may display bad patterns of behaviors in response to their adverse situations (e.g., yelling, bulling others, etc.). Their misconduct could trigger adverse reactions from other individuals, not just because of matters of disagreeing with the bad behavioral, but also because said wrongdoings could set bad examples for the younger generations.

Nevertheless, judging and criticizing folks for their misconduct is never the best way to tackle any trouble. Better approaches should include lending supportive and nonjudgmental assistance to people who are going through difficulties.

If the person making mistakes and bad choices is no other than yourself, stop for a moment and rethink your approaches. Give yourself a brake and remember that anyone could fall or stumble upon obstacles that might be blocking the road of life.

Therefore, stop wasting your time thinking about the things you have done while trying to cope with some nerve-racking situation. Rather, focus your attention and energy on trying to figure out what you could do better next time around. Then, decide what things can help you find your way out of your problems and do the right thing. Above all, remember, a positive attitude goes a long way.

Practical Application

Troubles and trials will always be around. Therefore, people must choose how to go about their situations and what to do with their lives. Troublesome situations are never welcome in people's lives.

For this reason, it is essential to learn how to troubleshoot bad situations to move forward in life. However, problem solving is a skill that not everybody has or can use.

Therefore, people can resort to getting help from good friends and relatives, which may be willing to help them figure out solutions for troubling situations.

Folks can also get help from doctors, lawyers, teachers, and professional counselors. They count among the long list of experienced persons have the expertise to help individuals to sort out some complex and critical situations.

Appeal

The approaches we choose to solve your problems can determine the outcomes of our troubling situations. Crumbling down in the midst of our problems is the wrong way to cope with them. Thankfully, there is always a positive path to problem solving.

Nowadays, folks can profit from the involvement or inputs from outsiders that can help individuals to figure things out and carry on with their plans. All these approaches are helpful.

However, based upon my personal experience, I can attest that having a confident faith in God can reenforce any troubleshooter we may choose to approach our situations.

The Lord does not spare us the troubles, but He is with us in the midst of them (Isaiah 41:10). With His help, we can cope with our situations in constructive ways that may ensure positive outcomes to our problems.

The Lord helped many people through the ages and continue to do it till this day. Have you come to Him for help?

*"Cast your cares on the Lord
and he will sustain you; he will never let
the righteous be shaken."*

- Psalms 55:22, NIV

POSITIVE WAYS OF COPING WITH FEARS AND DIFFICULTIES

Undoubtedly, sin has brought lots of troubles, sufferings, and distresses into the world. Bad things that may happen sudden or unexpectedly may crush people's plans and dreams. However, letting their problems bear them down has never help anyone solve any problem.

Contrarily, individuals who get up and keep on working on alternative solutions for their problems, are more likely to get good outcomes than those who collapse under the weight of their unwanted circumstances.

However, moving on despite of difficulties could prove to be a living nightmare, but a positive mindset can help individuals make it through their situations.

Here are some practical tips to cope with adversities while striving to find plausible solutions to overcome the difficulties.

a.) Be Optimistic

Whenever the roads of life get obstructed with trials and tribulations, positive-minded individuals must fight back and strive to find solutions for their problems. Having an optimistic mind can enable people to realize that despite its intricacies and difficulties, life is still worth living.

b.) Persevere

Nevertheless, a positive attitude is not the only attribute that will help folks attain victory over trials. In order to succeed in their endeavors, people must face their challenges with perseverance.

c.) Avoid Pessimism

People's character, personality, tendencies, and other personal attributes could be linked to their susceptibility to entertain dark thoughts. Regardless, individuals who struggle with rough circumstances should avoid giving in to their distresses and succumbing to their impulses.

Pessimistic stances can interfere with people's abilities to find new ways to get out of the problems that assault them. Therefore, they must be avoided at all cost.

d.) Readiness

People may struggle with many disturbing thoughts or situations that could steal away their mental and spiritual peace. Fortunately, there are many solutions to solve difficult problems and uncertain situations.

However, wallowing in their distresses and crying over their troubles and difficulties can hinder people's efforts to find the right solutions for their problems.

For this reason, individuals must nurture the willingness and readiness to get unstuck of troubling circumstances. This is a very important step that can help individuals solve their problems.

e.) Brainstorm Solutions

Problem solving requires planning. Therefore, the next important thing to do is brainstorming solutions. Whenever I am overwhelmed with troubling situations, my brain goes on freeze mode. Under those circumstances the only thing that works for me is taking some time out to clear up my mind.

After a short, or a long mental break, I am better able to establish my priorities to take care of my situations in order of importance. If I am ready, I start working on my solutions, otherwise, I take another mental break; then, I brainstorm my tactics, and finally, I implement them in order of priority. You could try this out too.

POSITIVE WAYS OF COPING WITH FEARS AND DIFFICULTIES

f.) Take Some Time Out

Depending on the person's state of mind, the process of solving a problem could be long or short, but at all times, individuals must make clever decisions to approach their situations.

This is why I like taking mental breaks before start brainstorming and implementing solutions for my problems. Taking mental breaks can help individuals clearer up their thoughts. Then, they will be able to make clever decisions and address difficult situations objectively.

Once they have reset the focus of their priorities, folks will be better able to start working on their projects, set deadlines, and start do their work in order of urgency or importance. This is a constructive way to keep on moving forward.

g.) Prioritize

When things get complicated, and there is a lot of physical or intellectual work to do, the best thing to do is to take some time out to clear up one's thoughts. Persons may have little or lots of things to do; but things would be much difficult for them if their minds are crowded with worries and troubles.

h.) Implement

After brainstorming solutions, deciding on a plan of action, and prioritizing their tasks, the next steps ahead is implementation. Proper execution of an action plan calls for individuals to sticking to that plan and carrying it through until the problem gets solved.

Sometimes, plans do work as expected. Whenever this happens, individuals must reexamine themselves and their plans, analyzing their circumstances to determine whether they need to replace or modify their original idea.

A good plan should meet the demands and the pace of the circumstances for which it was conceived. Therefore, it is important to be flexible and make room for better alternatives to be used if the plan ever needs modified or canceled out.

For instance, an office crew has to work with lots of clients, However, a public health crisis caused them to close their business. What should they do? They could modify their services and work remotely. This is an example of plan modification.

Here is another example. The success of a restaurant depends on the amount of client they work for each day. However, if they start losing clients on account of a health or economic crisis, this business may lose more money than what was spent.

Then, after considering their alternatives, the administrators might opt for going out of business to avoid losing more revenues. This is an example of plan cancelation.

i.) Get Help

There are some things that people might not be able to do on their own. They may need help brainstorming ideas or implementing plans, but they must take care of their businesses.

The best approach to these types of situations would be taking advantage of external resources to solve their problems. For examples, persons who need to pay taxes, may opt for hire a tax preparer to help them file their taxes.

Here is another example. A woman is overwhelmed with domestic duties could hire a maid to help with the housework, or a nanny to help caring for the children.

j.) Allow Others to Help You

There are some people, whose physical or mental impediments merits for them to get help from others. However, as awkward as it may seem, some of these individuals may feel that they could do things on their own.

These folks are prone to insist on refusing any help that it is offered to them. This may sound insane, but believe it or not, these kinds of things do happen.

I have met some of these individuals. Thus, I am aware that some people may need help because their mental or physical incapacity renders them unable to do these things any longer.

Several folks may lack the resources to carry out their duties efficiently; some others may just be too proud to get help from outsiders. Believe it or not, these situations are more common than we realize.

Fortunately, most people who need help actually want and can get it. Help is always around us. Therefore, people do not need to play hero to do things they can no longer do. Rather, folks should put shyness and pride aside and accept all the help available to them.

Practical Application

Think about everything you have read through and try to answer these questions:

- Do you know anybody who needs help with their problems?
- How about you? Have you ever needed anyone to help you brainstorm solutions for your problems?
- Are you among the goodhearted individuals that can help other people sort things out?
- Are you willing and able to help other people to find solutions for their problems?
- Think about your answers and remember that there are many alternative solutions for problem solving. Whether they do it themselves, or have external help, people can find their ways out of the situations that assault them.

Appeal

People's attitude and coping mechanisms play pivotal roles in finding solutions for their problems. For these reasons, I have assembled another set of insights that can empower you along your way.

- Remain calmed in the heat of adversities. This will enable you to think better in the middle of your troubles.

- Know who you are. Do not allow harsh situations define you. You can do the right thing without having to sacrifice your spiritual and moral values.
- Help others. Everybody has troubles of their own, but many individuals can help each other while brainstorm solutions for their own problems. Furthermore, on many instances, assisting the needy may also contribute to alleviate the problems of the ones who are lending the help to the needy person.
- Be grateful. Things could always get worse. Therefore, rather than complaining, individuals should be grateful for the things they have and even for what they do not have.

Remember, God knows us very well. He is aware of our situations and knows what we need. He will provide the resources and solutions for those needs. Thus, believe in Him and move forward in faith. This empowering attitude will give you courage to look forward to better things ahead. Do you believe this?

HOW TO OVERCOME FEARS THROUGH FAITH

Problems come and go, and as people strive to find solutions for their situations, their souls yearn for something better and more sublime than anything that the human mind could conceive.

Let us take King David's life as example. He was a man experienced in sorrows; but he always remembered to tell God about his problems and seek for His counseling. We can find plausible evidence of this practice embedded in all of his writings.

Notice the way in which David poured his soul before God in the following verse: *"Hear O Lord, when I cry with my voice, and be gracious to me and answer me"* (Psalm 27:7, NASB).

Another familiar plea of David's soul was *"Hear O Lord, when I cry with my voice, and be gracious to me and answer me"* (Psalm 27:7, NASB). The Lord never failed David. He always came through for David; He can do the same for every one of us too.

Today, David's pleas resemble the cry of millions of humans who long for the comfort and support of the Almighty. Are you one of them? Think of these things as you read through the following set of insights; they may help you succeed in your endeavors.

a.) Take a Hold of Yourself

Finally, if you ever find yourself struggling with dead-end-like situations put yourself together regardless of the turbulences. Be brave, remain strong, and never give up on your efforts. If you do not quit, sooner or later you will think of something that will help you get through your hardships.

b.) Make Room For Your Maker

Give Him the opportunity to rule over the destinies of your life, and you will taste and see His marvelous wonders. Then again, why is so important to give the Lord the opportunity to rule over our lives? What can He do to make things better for us?

Anyone who has ever undergone hardships has the potential to answer these questions because nothing replaces the practical experience. We can also go back in time and learn from the experiences of many ancient heroes of faith. They can enhance our ones in many different ways.

c.) Collaborate with the Lord

Once you are done organizing your thoughts, get ready to work things out, and believe that God Is with You. All things possible for Him. However, God does not want to do all the work alone. He wants us to work together with Him and be participants of His divine plan for our lives. If we team up with Him, He will show us the way to happiness, away from distress.

Believe in God's Promises

Let us keep it real: God did not promise to spare us the troubles; He promises to be with us in the midst of them. These are His words:

"*When you pass through the waters, I will be with you; and through the rivers, they will not overflow you, when you walk through the fire, you will not be scorched, nor will the flame burn you*" (Isaiah 43:2, NASB).

God's promises are faithful and true, and they are given to everyone, including people who claim that they do not care about God and that He does not care about them. People who harbor these thoughts in their hearts are wrong.

God cares about everyone because He is Love (1John 4:8); in other words, love is the essence of His character. The problem is that, often times, people do not care about God.

In the beginning, everybody worshiped one God: Elohim. However, as time went by, paganism made its entrance into the world and all the nations embraced it. However, the children of Israel, the descendants of Abraham, were the only ones who remained faithful to their Creator.

For this reason, God chose the descendants of Abraham as human instruments through which He could utter His Words of love and true unto all nations. Isaiah the prophet recorded this disposition in the following terms:

"It is I who have declared and saved and proclaimed, and there was no strange god among you; so, you are my witnesses, declares the Lord, and I am God.

Even from eternity I am He and there is none who can deliver out my hand; I act and who can reverse it?" (Isaiah 43:10, 11, NASB). *"Turn to me and be saved, all the ends of the earth; for I am God and there is no other"* (Isaiah 45:22, NASB).

As per these statements, God's Word is eternal and valid for all mankind. God used human instruments to bestow His words unto His children, and they engraved God's Words in scrolls, stones, and ultimately, in books (the Holy Scriptures).

These holy scriptures declare that: *"The grass withers, the flower fades, but the word of our God stands forever"* (Isaiah 40:8, NASB). For this reason, God's Word abides as faithful and true, even till these days. Believe this and enjoy the comfort, the grace, and the blessings of the God who loves and cares for you.

He is not only the God of the people who lived in Israel thousands of years ago. He is the God of all humanity. Patriarchs and Prophets, who lived thousands of years before us, were the instruments the Lord used to reveal His words to mankind; in It He tells us:

Also, the foreigners who join themselves to the Lord, to minister to Him, and to love the name of the Lord… and holds fast My covenant: even those I will bring to My holy mountain and make them joyful in My house of prayer. Their burnt offerings and their sacrifices will be acceptable on My altar; for My house will be called a house of prayer for all the peoples (Isaiah 56:6, 7, NASB).

Trust in God

While undergoing difficulties and needing God's guidance to face your problems, frustration and confusion might cause you to doubt God's Word, love, and power to help you overcome your worst situations.

Nevertheless, you must not dismay. Do not let setbacks define your beliefs or guide your intuitions. Know that, even though you do not see it, God is with you. He has always been by your side and will never leave you.

Thus, if the adversity in question involves a disease, know that God is able to help you with all your needs. He can perform miracles to heal your infirmities either directly, or through the hands of health care professionals, advisors, as well as friends and relatives who will work with you to nurse you back to a healthy state.

If the situation involves some legal matter, remember that God is able to fight your battles for you. He can change the course of the circumstances, and make justice shine through for you with a glow that could outshine the bright light of the day.

The Lord knows your circumstances and He can help you find the best way to solve your problems. If your problems are linked to something or someone who is making your life difficult, God can transform that hostility into harmony and peace.

Often times, God's will for people's lives can be revealed through the diligent efforts of lawyers, judges, and several other individuals, who work with the legal system to ensure that their rights do not get violated.

The Lord can make powerful impressions upon people's minds and transform them into better and more sensible individuals. Therefore, have faith, persevere in prayer, and you will see God working miracles on your behalf.

Personal Application

Sin has left us dealing with stormy situations and fierce difficulties that come our ways. However, God is awesome, merciful, faithful, and true. His has promised to be by our side. Therefore, He will never abandon us.

The Lord will help us with withstand the flood of situations that may threaten to drown us down. He will help us get through the fiery inferno of difficulties that may threaten to scorch our lives until we no longer exist.

The Lord draws us towards Him (John 12:32); yet He wants us to choose to be with Him voluntarily. Hence, God's call is also a promise of comfort and assurance for the weary soul: "*Come unto me all ye that labor and are heavy burdened, and I will give you rest*" (Matthew 11:28, KJV).

This biblical reference clearly state that God is a universal deity. His grace is sufficient to reach all the children of His creation, and His arms are open wide to embrace everyone, Jews, and gentiles.

Christians, Judaists, Muslims, Buddhists, Hindus, Mormons, unaffiliated, and everybody else in between, we all have been called by the Lord. He wants to save us all.

Therefore, you and I can confidently believe that the same God who helped millions and millions of people throughout the centuries is still able to extend His mighty hand to help you, me, and anybody who is willing to give Him a chance to rule the destinies of his or her life.

Appeal

Reader, entrust your situations onto God Almighty and He will guide your steps along the way. He will help you find solutions for your problems and will give you strengths to withstand the test of the circumstances.

The Lord is your God and mine. I have heard His call and believed His message. How about you? If you have not done it yet, I invite you to hear God's calling and believe in Him. Then, build a meaningful relationship with the Lord and be transformed by the power of His amazing Grace.

---

*"I will instruct you and teach you in the way
you should go;
I will counsel you with my eye upon you."*

- Psalms 32:8, ESV

FOLLOWING THE LEADING OF THE LORD

As we journey through this life, we need a personal guide to show us the way in which we should go. Without this type of help, we could easily get lost and confused in the trails of this life.

Thankfully, we already have a guide. He is our Lord and loving creator. According to the sacred scriptures, God loved us so much, *"that He gave His only begotten son, that whosoever believes in Him, shall not perish, but has everlasting life"* (John 3:16, NASB).

God does not want anyone to perish, but His wish is for everyone come to Him in repentance and be eternally saved. You may ask, why do people need to be saved? Then I would answer, because every one of us has sinned against God, and *"fallen short of His glory"* (Romans 3:23).

For this reason, the entire human race is subject to weaknesses, sufferings, and death. Nevertheless, God wants to give us His eternal and perfect life (Romans 6:23).

Then again, what is sin? Sin is the violation of God's laws, and the reason why we are constantly being oppressed by troubles and trials. However, God loves us so much, that He came down to us in the person of His son Jesus Christ to repair the damage caused by sin and give us all an opportunity to start anew.

God wants to have a personal relationship with you, me, and with the entire humanity. He wants to share His secrets with us. He wants to show us the ways in which we should walk. His tender voice is still saying: *"I will instruct you and teach you the way in which you shall go"* (Psalm 32:8, NASB).

The leading of the Lord is what we need the most when we have come to the end of the road and feel unable to see our way out. It is also what we need when we have done everything in our power to get things done right, just to realize that things just keep on worsening even more.

Have you ever experienced such burden? If so, I want you to know that you are not alone in the midst of your conflicts; amidst your most terrible moments, there is God.

The Lord is Almighty. Even though, He does not impose Himself onto us, but wants us to befriend Him voluntarily. He wants us to tell Him about our deepest secrets. Hence we must ask for His help and seek Him with faith.

God wants to protect and deliver us from troubles. He wants to supply for all our needs and wants us to be happy.

God gives us numerous opportunities to come to Him, but along with those opportunities comes the prerogative of making our own choices. This is how we tell the Lord: "come into my heart; take control of my life."

Then, the lord will guide and transform our lives into His likeness (2 Corinthians 3:18). This type of guidance requires submission from one person to another —or as Paul the apostle would say:

"As you have received Christ Jesus the Lord, so walk in Him" (Colossians 2:6, NASB). Are you walking in Christ's ways? If you do it, your spiritual life will grow in Him and He will share His secrets with you, because: *"The secret of the Lord is for those who fear Him, and He will make them know His covenant"* (Psalm 25:14, NASB).

How wonderful is to know that we, unfaithful beings can always count on a faithful God to lead and guide us along the way! He is always by our side, even when our actions do not fully agree with His will for our lives. He is always faithful.

FOLLOWING THE LEADING OF THE LORD

For as long as we love Him and obey His precepts, we will be able to discern His will for our lives and see Him in the ways He chooses to show Himself to us.

God can manifest Himself to us in many different ways:

God may send us dreams.

He may send messengers to minister to us on His behalf.

God can reach out to us via many other means that He regards as appropriate. God's guidance will get us through each challenge and every situation we may face. He will lead us to victory.

These things may sound too good to be truth, but they are true. Many biblical and nonbiblical accounts can assert this affirmation, e.g., the stories of Saul of Tarsus and Ananias – two men who learned the true meaning of being led by the Lord. Both narratives can attest of God's goodness and teach us valuable lessons for godly living. Please turn to the next chapter to read these stories.

*"The thief does not come except to steal, and to kill, and to destroy.
I have come that they may have life, and that they may have it more abundantly."*

- John 10:10, NKJV

SAUL: VINDICATOR OF GOD?

This narrative was originally recorded in the ninth chapter or the book of Acts of the Apostles. Its nineth chapter contains the narratives of two men who were devoted to "serving" God.

One of these men was a believer in Christ and follower of God's precepts. The other thought of himself as godly and righteous and his name was Saul of Tarsus. Saul's quest was vindicating God's name by all means possible.

However, there was a problem: Saul's efforts to attain this goal resulted in many wrongful doings both, in the eyes of God and men. Even so, God, which knows and understands all things, saw through Saul's motives and actions, and judged him wise and mercifully.

Throughout the span of his life, Saul had been taught about God. Hence, as he grew up, Saul vowed to serve Him unconditionally no matter the cost, and so it was.

Seizing after Christ's disciples was one of those extreme things. From his "godly" pharisaic standpoint, Saul was doing the "right" thing; the "zeal of the Lord "consumed" and "compelled" Saul to do everything that he did.

Nevertheless, nothing escapes the watchful eye of God. Thus, the Almighty One took notice of Saul's motives, and made arrangements for a personal encounter with him.

Like Saul, many believers across the centuries cannot see things as God sees them. Thus, many of them take matters into their own hands and done things according to their own perceptions, and not according to God's will for their lives. Let us now get back to the story.

Judging by the detailed information we have about him, it could be said that Saul was very serious about his calling. The young Pharisee had heard of Jesus; but he learned to obey God's precepts from the pharisaic point of view.

For this reason, Saul regarded Jesus as blasphemer, who was crucified for disturbing the peace of his people. Despite of all the facts that stood against their Leader However, why Jesus' followers kept on multiplying by the minute. This was a mystery that Saul could not understand

Nevertheless, Saul set out to do something drastic to vindicate God's name. Hence, he decided to destroy the disciples' creed, their reputation, as well as everything and anybody that could encourage others to follow that Jesus.

To that end, Saul engaged himself in the gruesome task of exterminating the Lord's followers. One day, as he was occupied on his grisly duty, Saul gathered some horsemen and headed off for Damascus.

He was so committed to his mission, that in his "zeal," Saul was practically breathing death threats against Jesus' disciples, and he had every intention to carry out said purpose against them.

Now, and before moving any further with this story, let us correlate Saul's beliefs and actions with the beliefs and behaviors of other religious people in these modern times.

First, notice that Saul's devotion to God led him to persecute and kill Jesus' followers. This does not seem to make sense, because godly people are supposed to love, not kill one another.

Second, it is highly unlikely that godly would people go out there in killing rampages, seizing other people in the name a God that could take care of himself if He really wanted. Do you get my point?

However, the same thing has happened these days as well. Many so called "godly people" still look down on other individuals who do not uphold the same creed and beliefs they have embraced. This unfortunate situation is leading numerous religious persons down a path similar to the one Saul of Tarsus took nearly two-thousand years ago.

Some of these believers go to the extremes of mutilating and killing themselves and others for the sake of defending their faith, religion, or cult. Personally, I do not think that this is God's will for any believer.

I think that God is powerful enough to defend Himself, and that, in His time, He can and will use anybody who humbly surrenders His life to Him, to do what, when, where, and how best pleases Him.

Additionally, the abundance of ambition and confusion in the world is causing people to do drastic and horrific things on account of their convictions. Many of these folks are literally wasting themselves away and exterminating others in the name of a god or for the sake of a cause.

Some people might not share my views on these things, and that is alright with me. People are entitled to have their own opinions, uphold their own beliefs, and do whatever they consider is best for them.

This explains why some people worship God while others worship idols or nothing at all (agnostics). This can also explain why there are so many different types of ideologies and doctrines that teach people about different rituals and deities and compel them to believe those types of things.

It is in light of these reasonings that I thank God for Saul's story. This narrative teaches us that not everybody who engages in violent acts that are linked to religious beliefs is actually a bad person.

Among them, there may be individuals who might be as mistaken as Saul was. He traveled the road to Damascus with the intention of killing as many Christians as possible. However, his Damascene experience tells us that, in spite of having killed so many disciples, Saul was not a criminal.

Saul was just a "committed" religious person who was trying to please God in his own way –the one he thought it was right. He did this for years, until the day he had a personal encounter with Jesus.

The day he journeyed to Damascus, Saul and his team were traveling to Damascus as fast they could. Saul could hardly wait to get started with such macabre mission; but he was completely unaware of the plans God had already ordained for him.

As they approached the city, the men were overcome by the appearance of the brightest light they had ever seen. Everybody stopped running and Saul fell to the ground. Then, the astonished men heard a great thundering sound; it was Jesus' voice.

Saul understood His words, but the rest of his men could only hear the sound of thunders. They could not recognize Jesus' voice because God's voice can only be recognized and understood by those who seek Him in spirit and in truth, and believe it or not, despite of his horrible past and present, Saul was one of them.

Paralyzed by confusion and still on the ground, Saul heard the Lord's voice saying: "Saul, Saul, why do you persecute me?"

"Who are you Lord?" – He asked.

"*I am Jesus whom you are persecuting*" (Acts 9:4, 5, NIV).

Jesus' declaration came as a shocking discovery for Saul of Tarsus. Suddenly, he become aware of his error.

Up until that moment, Saul had thought that he knew everything there was to know about God and His laws, but after being confronted by God Himself, Saul realized that he had to learn to know Him all over again.

Saul's experience left him physically blind; however, his spiritual eyes were wide open for the first time in his life.

After confronting Saul for his behavior, the Lord gave the young man specific instructions about the things he needed to do from then on. Saul did not question the Lord but acknowledged his need for guidance.

At last, Saul of Tarsus was ready to submit himself to the Lord and doing as He commanded.

ANANIAS, SERVANT OF GOD

Meanwhile, in the city of Damascus, a man named Ananias was also having an encounter with Jesus. The Lord came to this man in a dream (Acts 9:12) and told him that he needed to find Saul.

Can you imagine Ananias' reaction? How must have he felt after hearing that request? Imagine him! Even in the visions of the night, this faithful disciple knew about Saul.

He knew that the man was trouble for the nascent Christian community and discerned that Saul's journey to Damascus was a death sentence for them all. However, Ananias could not understand God's plan.

Judging by the narrative, I think that Ananias probably told himself: "How could the Lord ask me to meet with this enemy?" Nonetheless, the Lord had spoken, and Ananias knew that he had to obey.

He still could not bring himself to do what God had asked. Hence, Ananias felt that he had to say something. He had to find out why the Lord was sending him on a suicide mission. For this reason, Ananias he ventured to say:

"*I have heard many reports about this man, and all the harm he has done to your saints in Jerusalem. And he has come here with authority from the chief priests to arrests all who call on your name*" (Acts 9:13, NIV).

When pondering on these things, I think that Ananias should have listened to and obey Jesus' command at once. I am sure that Ananias knew this as well.

However, once you have a special relationship with God, you can dare to do things that others would never do. This is exactly what Ananias did. He dared to speak back to the Lord and inquire about His command.

Thus, Ananias questioned the Lord's command, and believe it or not, the Lord let Ananias do it. He listened to the concerns of his faithful servant.

This is another thing that I love about God. He is not just out there telling people what to do. He is also nearby readily open to dialogue with His children.

He is willing to listen to our suggestions and opinions, and ready to give them the assurance they need. This is exactly the way in which the Lord handled Ananias' concerns.

He told him: "*Go! This man is my chosen instrument to carry my name among the Gentiles and their kings and before the people of Israel*" (Acts 9:15, NIV).

Ananias trusted the Lord very much. Therefore, after hearing Jesus' words, this godly man carried out the instructions he had received.

Wow! God never ceases to amaze us! Did you notice what is going on here? Here He is, forgiving a man who dedicated his entire life to the gruesome task of hunting and killing Christians. Then, He chooses and appoints the same man to work for the cause he once seized and hated.

Isn't this a wonderful thing? How many of us would be willing to give a "traitor" a second chance? God did. He did it because He sees our actions and knows about the motives hiding behind those actions. He, who knows the motives and intentions of the heart knew that He could trust Saul.

Jesus knew that Saul was not a bad man after all. He knew despite his wrongful deeds, that Saul was just trying to apply the principles he had learned in the school of the Pharisees. He was sure that once Saul became convicted of the truth, he would fight for it until the very end, and so it was.

A PATHWAY TO LIVING A VICTORIOUS LIFE

Ananias submission to God's request teaches us about another principle that believers must incorporate in their lives and is this: once a person gets convicted to doing God's will, this person must surrender to Him and follow through with the plans the Lord has for his or her life.

Hence, if we want to do the will of the Lord, but do not fully understand His will for our lives, all we have to do is pray, like Ananias did. We must also be obedient to the Lord and wait upon His love. If we persevere in faith, in due season, God will make all things clear for us. Then, we will be able to understand the things that at the moment we cannot comprehend.

Saul and Ananias were two men devoted to the Lord. Although they had committed their lives to an analogous purpose, these two men carried out their actions in totally opposite ways.

However, the God who knows who we are, what is in our mind, what we did, what we are doing, and what we will do, knows how to help us through. He also knew what to do with the lives of Saul and Ananias. Is not this a wonderful thing?

Perhaps, as you are reading through these lines through, you are trying to decide whether to receive God's favor. If this were the case, then, all you have to do is to trust in Him.

Find your delight in the Lord, "and He will give you the desires of your heart. Commit your ways to the Lord, and He will do it, He will bring forth your righteousness as the light and your judgment as the noonday. Rest in the Lord and wait patiently in Him" (Psalm 37:3-7, NASB).

This is the secret of living in victory. Trust the Lord with all your affairs. Be certain that He will share His secrets with you as He does with everyone who fears and obey Him. This makes plenty of sense, doesn't it?

Think about this, would you share your secrets with strangers? Would you try to help people who are neither seeking nor asking for your help? That would be an intrusion, wouldn't it? God is like that too. He will only guide those who submit themselves to Him.

Practical Application

"The secret of the Lord is for those who fear Him, and He will make them know His covenant" (Psalms 25:14, NASB).

If you trust in God, if you commit your ways onto Him, He will take care of everything for you. He will take care of you finances, relationships, health, future plans and projects, and everything else that matters to you.

Delve deep inside your soul and a think about the situations that trouble you. How are you handling them? Are you fighting God's battles for Him, or are you willing to give the Lord the opportunity to change the course of your life?

I do not know what your answer to those questions would be; but this I know, God is always ready, willing, and able to lead and guide those who trust him with everything that goes on in their lives. He did it with Ananias and Saul. He will also lead anyone who is willing to be guided by Him.

A PATHWAY TO LIVING A VICTORIOUS LIFE

Appeal

God gave Ananias specific instructions concerning things that must be done. He did the same with so many other people throughout the centuries. He is the ruler of my life and wants to be yours as well. Would you give Him a chance to be the ruler of your heart?

May you say yes to the Lord and may your grateful soul lift its voice in blissful worship, singing: *"I will bless the Lord who has counseled me; indeed, my mind instructs me in the night. I have set the Lord continually before me; because He is at my right hand I will not be shaken"* (Psalm 16:7-8, NASB).

May this assurance abide with you forever that you may always remember that the Lord is with you every step of the way. Rest upon the confidence of His peace.

The break of dawn proclaims the end of darkness and the beginning of a brand new day filled with endless possibilities.

Photo courtesy of the author

*"For He will give His angels orders
concerning you,
To protect you in all your ways."*

- Psalm 91:11, NASB

ENCOUNTER WITH ANGELS

So far, we have been scrutinizing many challenging things that can happen to people and how can individuals overcome their difficulties. Now, as we move on with this conversation, let us go over a story that can help us highlight the willingness and power God to help His children.

Jacob: A Treacherous Fugitive

Have you ever heard the expression "the God of Abraham, Isaac and Jacob"? Do you know where this phrase came from? It came from the personal experiences of those ancient Patriarchs. The relationship these men had with their Maker, and the legacy they left behind, has benefited many believers back in their days, as well as and millions of believers who lived after them.

Up until today, the testimony of those Patriarchs continues to be a source of inspiration for those who believe in the Lord even until these days. Each time any of those Patriarchs went through something, they called upon the name of the Lord and He answered them.

This prayful attitude amidst the difficulties was one of their secret weapons to overcome adversity. We can learn lots of good things from their experiences. For this reason, let us now analyze a selected portion of the story of Jacob, the Patriarch, Abraham's grandson.

After the death of his grandfather Abraham, Jacob deceived his father to receive a special blessing that belonged to his older brother, Esau. However, Jacob's deceitful deed infuriated his brother Esau. Therefore, obeying his mother's instructions, Jacob was forced to flee from his home and went off to live with his mother's relatives.

Thus, Jacob headed off for Paddam-aram, the land of his parents and the place where he would live with his uncle Laban form then on. That day and that journey marked the beginning of Jacob's relationship with God.

The price that Jacob had to pay for his wrongful actions was rather high, for he was forced to run for his life. Perhaps, he was sorry for having deceived his father and stolen his brother's blessings; but it was too late for regrets.

The hope of ever seeing his parents alive again had swiftly vanished away, and Jacob had to face the consequences of his wrongdoings. Jacob's mind was flooded with many thoughts and memories that were left behind in the land that saw his birth.

In his oblivion, Jacob was totally unaware that he was not alone in his journey; somebody was watching over him. The road ahead was a path of danger and uncertainties. As he traveled along, Jacob had to struggle with feelings of sadness, guilt, fear, loneliness, among others. He reflected on his past, and grieved for the mistakes he had made, but kept on moving on.

The night was fast approaching; knowing that he would have to take a break until dawn, Jacob found a quiet spot, chose the right rock, laid his head down on it, and fell asleep. Then, the One who had been watching over him, came to Jacob in a dream.

That night, Jacob dreamed of a ladder that had its base on the ground and a top that reached up to the sky. The young man was elated by the celestial vision. In it, Jacob which watched angels ascending and descending on the ladder, and the Lord standing above its top. Suddenly, he heard a voice that told him:

"I am the Lord, the God of your father Abraham, and the God of Isaac; the land on which you lie, I will give it to you and to your descendants. Your descendants will also be like the dust of the earth, and you will spread out to

the west and to the east and to the north and to the south, and in you and your descendants shall all the families of the earth be blessed. Behold, I am with you and will keep you wherever you go" (Genesis 28:12-15, NASB).

Let us pause here for a moment.

Did you notice how the Lord approached this fugitive man, who had dealt treacherously with his closest relatives? Notice how God without minding his sinful past, God gave Jacob the assurance of His presence.

Right then and there, his experience made Jacob realize that he was not alone. He had been told about the Lord throughout his life, but that night, Jacob had the privilege of beholding God's majesty. This nightly experience comforted Jacob's guilty soul and gave him courage to keep on moving on.

At the break of dawn Jacob set himself to travel the road ahead of him. The treacherous road warned Jacob of the many dangers he would have to face. However, he would have to keep on moving forward like his father Isaac and his grandfather Abraham did it back in their days.

Distress and fear took the hold of Jacob, but his nightly experience helped him develop a personal relationship with God. He overcame the dangers he encountered on his path to the land of his ancestors. Several days later, Jacob arrived to Padam-aram, the land of his mother.

He managed to mingle with his relatives and grow as a person. In that land, Jacob met his cousin Rachel and got married, and started a family. Years later, he decided to stop hiding from his past and returned to the land of his parents.

Therefore, Jacob left Padam-aram and started off his journey back to Canaan. When they were approaching Canaanite's territory, Jacob was told that his brother Esau was on his way to meet him.

Then, Jacob's heart trembled with fear. He remembered what he had taken away from his brother and feared for his life. Hence, he worked out a plan to soothe his brother's anger and make up with him.

However, despite his most diligent efforts, Jacob's desperate soul could not remain at peace, nor could the cry of his guilty spirit be quenched. Thus, in his anguish, Jacob sought the favor of the Lord in fervent prayer and supplication; after that night, his night would never be the same again.

Jacob's action of asking the Lord for help resulted in a personal encounter with His Maker. On that night, Jacob fought with a powerful angel till the break of dawn.

I imagine that while they were fighting, the angel was letting Jacob hope for victory. However, just before dawn, the angel gave Jacob a small taste of his celestial power.

Then, acknowledging that he had a big disadvantage in that fight, Jacob stopped fighting, but held on to the angel as tight as he could. The angel asked Jacob to let go of him. However, Jacob refused to let go.

That angel was Jacob's best chance of obtaining triumph over his brother. Hence, he persisted on holding him tight. Again, I imagine that the angel let Jacob have that one too; but once showtime was over, and Jacob had learned his lesson, the angel blessed Jacob and he finished his journey in peace.

He knew that everything would be alright. His fears had vanished, and he was finally ready to make peace with his brother.

Practical Application

Jacob's story encodes the message we have been trying to bring across this entire book all along – the reality and the power of a God that can lift us up when we are down and give us new strengths to travel the road ahead despite its disadvantages.

God watches over all His creatures, including individuals who wonder away in the mist of their struggles. Today, anyone who, like Jacob, works out the courage to face guilts and fears will have to hold on tight to the Lord too.

Anyone who seeks divine protection and forgiveness from the Lord, will not be disappointed by Him. Like Jacob, we all have a story to tell because we all have gone through some tough times at some point in our lives.

However, we too can be overcomers like Jacob. We too can hold on tight to the Lord until He gives us strength, courage, and blessed hopes for triumphant living.

Therefore, let take all our concerns to the Lord in prayer. Let us wrestle with Him until He grants us the blessings we need to keep on moving forward.

Appeal

Friend, if like Jacob, you too have done things you do not feel proud of; but can find peace and redemption from your wrongdoings by way of having a one-on-one battle with the Lord in prayer.

He will reason with you, forgive your sins, and help your soul find strength in Him. Just trust in God's promises, and you will find spiritual rest in His everlasting arms.

"Those who look to him are radiant; their faces are never covered with shame."

- Psalms 34:5, NIV

DAVID'S – A LIFE OF STRIVES AND TRIUMPH

However, God is always walking alongside those who love Him and keep His commandments and blesses them in many different ways. Hence, let us scrutinize this topic a little deeper that we may have a small taste of the goodness of God.

To that end, let us move on with an analysis of some portions of the story of another great pillar of faith in biblical times. Let us talk about David, the humble boy who became king of Israel.

As a child, David was a shepherd boy, who loved his family and was very devoted to his God. His main responsibility was tending the family's sheep herd –a task that he performed each day with great pleasure and courage.

Since he worked on the fields each day, this young shepherd was not stranger to danger. Often times, wild animals (e.g., bears and mountain lions) threatened his safety or that of his sheep. However, David always found a clever way to manage any dangerous situation.

Thus, the shepherd boy defended himself and his flock from any wild beasts that dared to attack them. His relationship with the Lord grew very tall with the passing of time, and David found a friend and protector in the Lord.

For this reason, David was constantly meditating in the Lord, and worshipped Him in every way he could. Whenever David's eyes were delighted to contemplate God's creation, he found inspiration for his poems in just about anything around him.

David wasted no time or opportunity to worship His friend God and talk with Him through Him in humble prayer. Worshiping the Lord was something that made David feel very happy.

David knew that worshiping the Lord God was the right thing to do. For David, worshipping God was a great pleasure. He knew the difference between worshiping the true God versus revering the idols venerated by other neighboring nations.

For this brave young man, those idols were just pieces of logs and stones with no power of their own. Thus, when considering his choices, David resolved to give God the first place in his life and decided that he would give everything up for the sake of the Lord.

More than a mere deity, God was David's everything. The Lord was David's most valued treasure, deliverer, and the only thing that truly mattered in life. His leaped with joy each time he contemplated the awesomeness of God through the book of nature.

No treasures in his kingdom would ever be compared to the fortune of having the Lord on his side. On one occasion, while meditating about his feelings towards God David said:

"*The Lord is the portion of my inheritance and the One who supported my lot*" (Psalm 16:5, NASB, paraphrased).

That is how highly David thought of the Lord and found his delight in worshiping his Maker. This devotion for God did not die off with the pass of time. Contrarily, it got stronger every day.

One day, Samuel the Prophet visited David's house and told the young shepherd's father that God had instructed him to anoint one of his children as the future King of Israel.

David's father felt honored by the prophet's statement and introduced the prophet to each one of David's brothers to Samuel; but none of them was chosen.

Finally, Samuel asked Isai – David's father, whether there were any more children he should meet with. Isai did not think that God would care to think of David as the future king of Israel.

Nevertheless, the elderly man sent for his youngest son that he could meet with the prophet. As soon as he saw him, Samuel, the prophet knew that David was the man God had chosen to lead Israel.

Thus, the godly prophet anointed David as future monarch of his nation. There would pass many years before David was publicly crowned as King and sat in his throne to rule the nation that saw his birth.

In the interim, young David grew up and he became a mighty worrier. His relationship with God grew very close and his life was filled with the joy of God's salvation. David worshiped, befriended, and trusted with all his hearts.

Nevertheless, despite this idyllic spiritual experience, David's life was not always as sweet as honey. The Bible tells us that, in addition to worshiping God, writing psalms, singing, and dancing for the Lord, David's life was also filled with conflicts and hassles that lasted throughout his entire life.

On one occasion, David went off to visit his brothers which were serving his country at the war zone. There, David noticed that the soldiers were in despair and tried to find out what was going on. His curiosity was satisfied when he learned that a certain Philistine giant kept on daring the Israelite army to fight with him.

Nonetheless, given their disadvantage in size and strength, none of the soldiers dared to accept the Philistine's challenge. When David became aware of this situation, the zeal of the Lord caused him to accept the challenge of fighting the giant (1Samuel chapter 17).

David did not accept the Philistine's dare because he trusted in his own strength and skills, but because he trusted in God's power to save him and his people from their enemies. Thus, David fought with the giant and won the battle because God was with him.

After that day, the young warrior was honored as a hero by his people, and despised like a rat by jealous king Saul, which hunted by him like a wild beast (1Samuel 26:20).

David underwent a host of serious problems that made him vulnerable to emotional pain and fears. King Saul was jealous of David's audace and seized him for many years (1 Samuel chapters 19 – 23).

This prickly situation forced David to hide away in the mountains, where he stayed until his evil foe, King Saul died in the heat of another battle field (1 Samuel chapter 31).

Throughout his years of pilgrimage, David's faith in the Lord caused him to embrace the constant assurance and trust in the Lord. God never led His faithful servant down. Through it all, God upheld, kept him, and saved him out of all his troubles.

Practical Application

David's mountain years caused him to feel trapped and tied up by his circumstances. With no way out, David refused to lose his faith in God. He fought many battles and won many victories because the Lord was always by David's side.

Time after time David south for the Lord's guidance and deliverance; and time after time, he got his wish in reward to his faith (Psalms 34:4). This should be the experience of anyone who professes to love the Lord.

Claiming to believe in God and attending Church every week is not good enough. Like David, it is imperative that believers find their delight in the Lord through meaningful worship, not just mere attendance to church's services. This is the kind of worship that God deserves to receive from His people.

David's ordeals and worship experiences may also help us understand the true meaning of his declaration:

"The Lord is the portion of my inheritance and my cup; "You support my lot. The lines have fallen to me in pleasant places; indeed, my heritage is beautiful to me" (Psalms 16:5, 6 NASB). This should be the language of anyone who has learned to walk with God and experienced His power to deliver from evil.

Today, David's testimonies constitute a powerful evidence of God's power to deliver His people from their tribulations. All we need to do is trust in God like David did, and the Lord will not betray that trust.

God delivered David from many dangers and helped him feel safe in times of troubles. The ancient monarch knew that for as long as he trusted in the Lord, there would be no more hiding, no more ties, no more fears that could hurdled him down.

The example he left behind is a plausible evidence that stresses the importance of learning to abide under the wings of the Almighty and find refuge in the shelter of the Most High (Psalm 91:1).

Appeal

Yes, God wants to set people free from their burdens. His loving offer to the human race is: *"Come to me, all who are weary and heavy-laden, and I will give you rest"* (Matthew 11:29, NASB). This is the Master's calling to those who need His help, Hence, He invites you to come onto Him and abandon your burdens at His feet.

Coming to the Lord in total surrender is also the best path to finding the strength needed to make it through the challenges till the very end and become an inspiration for others.

God loves you and wants to help you live more abundantly. Therefore, He offers you His gifts of joy and peace that will displace the sorrows away. Hear His comforting voice still saying:

"Peace I leave with you, my peace I give to you; not as the world gives do I give to you. Do not let your heart be trouble, nor let it be fearful" (John 14:27, NASB).

Thus, if you have not done it yet, accept the Lord's invitation to come to Him. Learn to experience true freedom in the shelter of the Almighty.

Have faith in the Lord. Abide in Him, and He will help you overcome your worst situations and will grant you His peace.

Photo courtesy of the author

"Have I not commanded you? Be strong and courageous. Do not be afraid; do not be discouraged, for the Lord your God will be with you wherever you go."

- Joshua 1:9, NIV

IN ALL YOUR SITUATIONS

a.) Our Raw Reality

While undergoing harsh tribulations many folks make efforts to try look fine in the outside and be strong in the inside. These individuals carry themselves out with such grace, that the people around them could hardly guess the kinds of situations they are going through, or the types of struggle they have.

Millions of people out there, bear the weight of many problems, afflictions, and difficulties. These persons may bear the unspeakable heaviness of weaken spirit. Their souls might be weary, worn out, and almost dismaying, but they just press on and move forward.

As they fight to conquer their adversities and get their breakthroughs, many of them may get a break when their efforts pay off. These folks count among the people who find solutions for their problems and get out of their situations with a smile in their faces.

Unfortunately, not every afflicted or weary person is ever able to get this desired outcome to troubling situations. Fair or not, there are millions of people who also go through life, fighting their battles and bearing their burdens with courage.

Many of these folks eventually lose their battles against their bad situations (e.g., illness, financial, legal issues, etc.), but their altruistic spirit refuse to give up in the midst of their ordeals.

These folks are heroes of life, which make the best of their adversities and keep on moving forward. Their attitudes are in ample contrast with the ones who crumble down under the weight of their terrible situations. This latter group may need plenty of emotional and social help from a variety of caring people.

b.) The Silver Lining

Certainly, many bad things that happen to people, can devastate their lives, and mutilate their hopes for the future. However, optimistic folks may be hurdled down by their difficulties, but will let their troubles define or defeat them.

Faith and courage empower folks to endure and overcome their difficulties. Hence, valiant, and optimistic souls will do everything in their power to triumph over their troubles and find the peace and comfort that have been made available to them.

You and I could be among those courageous individuals who fight their battles triumphantly. Therefore, quitting all dismay and discouragement, let us remember that God is by our side, helping us get through all our situations.

Like David, we too can choose to believe that the Lord is our portion and the One who sustains, delivers, and guides us always, especially in times of difficulties. Let us also believe that the Lord will give us renewed strengths to overcome our hurdles.

Then, we will see the mighty hand of God working miracles in our lives. We will be pleased to see the way things will turn up and will no longer feel tied up by our circumstances. Contrarily, our souls will find rest in the confident assurance of the Most High.

Personal Application

Chances are that as you read these lines through, you might be struggling with some heavy burdens. Perhaps you are trying to save a marriage or dealing with a broken one.

You might be struggling to raise your children well and instruct and guide them in their way. Then, you come to realize that your offspring just want to be left alone to follow after their own instincts and do whatever they want.

Perhaps you unemployed or seeking for a better job, while mountains of bills and problems pile up by the minute. You might be trying to keep up with payments and other financial burdens or have opted for taking things one day at the time while looking forward to uncertain outcomes ahead.

Perhaps you are in an abusive relationship, hoping for the best, but fearing the worse. The hopes for good changes keep you going, but your reality remains a mystery for you and your loved ones.

Perhaps you live in a bad neighborhood, where crime and violence are just around the corner. You may want to move to a safer place, but your income and circumstances may not allow you to do so.

Perhaps you have been victim of bias or segregation of any nature. Perhaps you have been ridiculed and abused by other people. You may have wanted to defend yourself against your opponents but did not dare to speak up about the unfair things that have happened to you or around you.

Perhaps, you are having a hard time staying away from friends who may want you to join them in doing things that conflict with your faith and moral values.

Perhaps you have been trying to keep up with your work responsibilities or getting good grades at school. However, the challenges of keeping up with peer pressure may compete with your abilities to perform well.

Perhaps, perhaps, perhaps… there are so many others perhaps. Which ones are yours?

While you try to answer these questions, know that the Lord can empower everybody to find solutions for their problems. His promises are applicable to every situation, including circumstances that were brought up by mistakes that have caused harm to self or others.

God can comfort the souls of people who have been hurt or have hurt others. He can ease our anxieties and vanish our guilts and sorrows. Hence, we can trust Him with our problems at all times, especially the difficult ones.

Those who love the Lord will not be tied up by the circumstances for long. "Their lines" will fall down in pleasant places, and God will make sure that they get double or triple for their losses.

Appeal

The Lord knows what you are going through, and He has a promise for every situation. He is your Helper and mine. If you trust Him with all your heart, if you give him all your worries and troubles, if you wait upon Him and embrace His promises, you will surely see Him coming through for you.

God is with you in the midst of your struggles. Rest upon His bosom whenever you feel weary. He is your friend, the mender of every brokenhearted, and the answer to all the needs and cares of every grieving soul.

Henceforth, do not wallow on the misery of a broken spirit. Remember that when your heart feels shattered, when the whole world comes crashing down on you, and you strive to find happiness in the midst of your sorrows, God is still with you. He can dry your tears away and give you confident assurance for better things to come.

Be certain that there will always be hope for better days ahead. God is always with you. Be strong and courageous and trust in the Lord. Know that in time, the pain will pass, and you will be alright.

The Almighty One walks along by your side. He wants to uphold you, guide you, strengthen, and comfort you. He wants to give you happiness and peace of mind and heart.

The day will come when the Lord will "wipe away every tear… and there will be no longer any death; there will be no longer any mourning, or crying, or pain" (Revelation 21:4, NASB). Then, your tears will turn into laughers, and you will be able to sing for joy again.

Meanwhile, let us have faith in Him and trust in His promises. They are like a blank check placed in your hands but redeeming that "check" is totally up to you. You decide whether you "cash it out" or put it in a drawer.

I have cashed out the check of these divine promises many times. Hence, based upon my personal experience I can attest that God's promises have kept me strong in the middle of my worst situations. For this reason, I dare to encourage you to cash that check now and experience the joy of the Lord!

*"Yes, and from ancient days I am he.
No one can deliver out of my hand.
When I act, who can reverse it?"*

- Isaiah 43:13, NIV

A MIGHTY HELP IN TIMES OF TROUBLES

People frequently go through unwanted situations that may disrupt the harmony of their lives. The troubles and trials that assail them daily have caused many individuals to feel tied up all over. While striving to overcome their difficulties, most people try doing their best to survive and thrive individually and collectively.

Surely, life is complicated. This is a reality that no one can deny. This realization might have been one of things that prompted King Solomon to meditate upon many things that happen in life and write the following words:

There is a time for everything, and a season for every *activity under the heaven:*

> *A time to be born and a time to die, a time to*
> *plant and a time to uproot,*
> *A time to kill and a time to heal, a time to tear*
> *down and a time to build,*
> *A time to weep and a time to laugh, a time to*
> *mourn and a time to dance,*

> *A time to scatter stones and a time to gather them, a time to embrace and a time to refrain, A time to search and a time to give up, a time to keep and a time to throw away, A time to tear and a time to mend, a time to be silent and a time to speak, A time to love and a time to hate, a time for war and a time for peace'*
> *...I thought in my heart, 'God will bring to judgment both the righteous and the wicked for there will be time for every activity and a time for every deed' (Ecclesiastes 3:1-8, 17, NIV).*

This profound set of words, wise King Solomon started his discourse on the facts of life. To this day, his words stand tall as practical truths that transcend the confinements of time.

Indeed, there is an appointed time for everything that takes place under the sun. Who can deny the veracity of these words? Just think about the many things, good and bad, that can shape our lives on a daily basis.

Some things could be very pleasurable. They can bring happiness into people's lives. These things are generally regarded as precious treasures upon which nobody could ever put a price tag.

However, there are also many sad and terrible things and situations, which sooner or later could disrupt the harmony of people's lives. The advent of these things may have impacting and devastating consequences on the lives of all the individuals who get affected by them.

Fortunately, God has already made provision for the unexpected. He uses different avenues and channels to convey assistance to every needy soul. Hence, hope is always around us.

The Lord is an expert in making circumstances work on behalf of those who love and trust Him. He has many different ways and resources to alleviate the needs of families undergoing difficulties. In fact, the Lord can use anyone and anything as an instrument to deliver His grace onto His children and free them from their troubles.

A MIGHTY HELP IN TIMES OF TROUBLES

The Lord has promised to be there with His children in the midst of their troubles (Isaias 41:10). Therefore, you and I are not alone in the midst of our distresses. God is with us! His promises are faithful and truth. Hence, you can claim them as your own. You can count on that.

God will take care of you because He loves you. *"He will bring forth your righteousness as the light and your judgment as the noonday. Rest in the Lord and wait patiently in Him"* (Psalm 37:3-7, NASB).

Surely, life could be difficult for a while, but things will not be bad not forever. The day will come, when everything will be set and done, and you will be delivered from the circumstances that had previously tied you up.

On that day, you must remember to be grateful. Give God the offering of your praise and He will show you His wonders. Therefore, I dare you to withstand the test of your adverse circumstances and make the habit of finding your delight in the Lord.

Believe in His promises because He is faithful to carry you through your difficulties. Stand strong and know that the Lord can grant your heart's desires. Henceforth, trust your affairs to the Lord.

"Commit your ways to the Lord and trust Him." Let Him handle all your troubles. Trust Him with your plans, your ways, the people in your life, and everything that concerns you. Then, worry no more. Consider things done, and He will take care of your affairs for you!

These statements may seem "too good to be true," but they are true. I can attest of their validity. For me, rather than beautiful fallacies, these words of affirmation are a wonderful reality. They are the expression of my deepest hopes in what the Lord can do for His children.

Believe me, I am a living example of what God can do in the lives of His children. The Lord has done so much for me! I remember so many occasions in which the Lord took time to think of me.

The Lord has comforted my heart when it was weary, made me feel His presence when I was in trouble, and guided me along the way. Hence, receiving His guidance beforehand has given me confidence to move forward.

Knowing that God walks alongside with me moment by moment, makes me feel very special every day of my life. Thus, having been a beneficiary of His goodness, I feel very loved and blessed by Him.

Therefore, I am not shy to say like David, "*I bless the Lord who has counseled me; indeed, my mind instructs me in the night. I have set the Lord continually before me; because He is at my right hand I will not be shaken. Therefore, my heart is glad, and my glory rejoices; my flesh also will dwell securely*" (Psalm 16:7-9, NASB).

Practical Application

This is the theme of my soul. How about you? Do you believe these things? Do you believe that the Lord will come through for you in the midst of your troubles? I hope you do.

However, if lack this blessed confidence and want the Lord to make a difference in your life, all you have to do is to claim His promises and stand by them. Then, your life will experience God's wondrous working power, and will praise the Lord like David saying:

"*I will bless the Lord at all times; His praise shall continually be in my mouth. My soul will make boast in the Lord; the humble will hear it and rejoice. O magnify the Lord with me and let us exalt His name together*" (Psalm 34: 1-3, NASB).

Appeal

Indeed, there is a time and a season for everything that happens under the sun. Let us enjoy the good things in good season, alongside with our loved ones.

Let us also withstand the bad seasons in our lives and endure the bad things that happen to us with courage and determination. Let our lips proclaim the Lord's name.

Let others see Him working miracles in your life and hear the words of your testimony. Perhaps they will turn to the Lord and bless His magnificent name. Are you up for this challenge?

A FAITHFUL GUIDE ALONG THE WAY

People are prone to go through and endure many difficult situations each day. However, no one has ever suffered as much as Jesus Christ. He loved, taught, helped, and healed many people, yet was rejected by them.

During His earthly life, Christ, the Lord was the subject of abuse and betrayal (Matthew 26:46-50) at the hands of the very people He ministered to. The bitterness of Christ's suffering was foretold by Isaiah the Prophet (Isaiah 53).

Thus, according to that prophecy, Jesus was smitten, stricken, and afflicted for us. The *"punishment that brought us peace was upon Him, and by His wounds we are healed"* (Isaiah 53:4, 5 NIV). He suffered the death of a criminal (Mark 15: 8-37). However, three days later, fulfilling the scriptures (Luke 24: 34-48), and overcoming the odds, the Lord rouse up from the dead (Matthew 28: 1-8).

Today, Jesus is near His people (Matthew 28:20). His suffering enabled Him to empathize with ours (Hebrews 4:15). Hence, Jesus helps everyone who struggles with troubles and trials (Isaiah 41:13).

Indeed, the Lord never abandons His children; rather, He reassures them with the promises of His Word. Take a look at these promises:

"Many are the afflictions of the righteous, but the Lord delivers him out of them all" (Psalm 37:19, NASB). *"If the Lord delights in a man's way, He makes his steps firm; though he stumbles, he will not fall, for the Lord*

upholds him with His hand. I was young and now I am old, yet I have never seen the righteous forsaken or their children begging bread" (Psalm 37:23-25, NIV).

Surely, the curse of sin brought forth tons of sorrows and tragedies in the world. The heart of the Father ached for our sufferings because He loves us. The sacred word says that "*God so loved the world, that He sent His Son into this world that through Him the world may be saved*" (John 3:16, 17, KJV).

This is the true reason that brought Jesus onto this Earth. He was born as a human, lived like a human, and walked the roads of human's sorrows and unwanted situations. Then, as mysterious as this may seem, Jesus conquered evil on our behalf by taking men's place in the cross.

The Lord Understands

Jesus can understand our feelings and identify Himself with our circumstances. The Lord empathizes with our afflictions because He has been acquainted with them before us.

The One who said, "*Foxes have holes and birds of the air have nests, but the Son of Man has no place to lay His head*" (Matthew 8:20, NIV), knows the meaning of not having a place to call home. However, rather than focusing on His own situations, Jesus traveled the roads of many cities.

During His earthly journey, Jesus had personal encounters with many sick people had mercy on them and healed them (Matthew 9: 36). He did it back then and can still do the same for us today.

Jesus can heal our infirmities and soothe our deepest sorrows, because He bore man's griefs on Himself, and carried our sorrows for us. Because of His sacrifice everyone now has the hope of abundant life in Him.

On the gloomy night prior to His sacrifice, the Lord experienced the burden of our sins, sorrows and struggles in His own flesh. His heart was heavy, and His spirit was broken. The anxiety that pierced His heart caused His bloody sweat damped the grassy ground.

Jesus could have used His divine powers to relieve His personal and emotional needs, but He opted for depending on His heavenly Father. Thus, Jesus knelt down and called upon the Father and asked for His help (Mathew 26:39).

Nevertheless, this time around, the Father did not grant His Son's request. Such act would have prevented the Son of God from fully empathizing with the sufferings of us humans, deprived of divinity. Hence, that sorrowful night, Jesus had to endure His distresses alone (Luke 22: 40 -45).

Luke registered his account of this story with the following words: "*He withdrew about a stone's throw beyond them, knelt down and prayed saying, 'Father, if you are willing take this cup from Me, yet, not my will, but Yours be done'. Now, an angel from heaven appeared to Him and strengthened Him*" (Luke 22:43, 44, NASB).

The presence of the angels that His Father had sent from above, empowered the Son to go through His agony and overcome evil. Now, His victory is our warranty that like Him, we too can be overcomers.

God did not spare Jesus from His sorrows, but was there for Him, empowering to overcome His difficulties. God can do the same for us today.

The Father would have loved to be with Jesus in that Garden. Nevertheless, this was Christ's battle field; the place and time when He bore our transgressions upon His shoulders for the sake of our salvation.

Thus, Jesus had to go through the pain alone that He might bear the burdens of the sinner race that He came to save. Knowing all these things, Jesus' human nature quaked inside Him.

The mere thought of the things He was about to endure filled the Lord's heart with anguish (Matthew 26:29). Therefore, Jesus entrusted His fate into the hands of His Father and was not disappointed by Him.

We too can entrust our problems to the Father. He understands every one of our thoughts and feelings, and as certain as He sent His holy angel to serve and comfort His beloved son, He will send His angels to minister to us, and His messengers will comfort and help us in troubling times.

Practical Application

Trusting God in the middle of our difficulties is a choice that every one of us has to make sooner or later. Even Jesus, the Son of God did not hesitate to trust in His Father throughout the span of His short human life.

For this reason, I dare to ask you to ponder upon your current condition; look in the back of your mind and try to find out what is wrong with you. Search inside your heart and determine what kinds of circumstances are besetting you today.

Quiz yourself and find out how do you feel in the midst of your distress? What do you do when things go wrong, and your plans fall apart? Can you have the confidence of David and boldly say: "The Lord is the portion of my inheritance and my cup (Psalm 16:5, NASB)?"

Can you stay strong in faith and look at the future with certainty in spite of the chaos? I hope so. Then, like David, you too will be able to boldly say: "the lines have fallen to me in pleasant places; indeed, my heritage is beautiful to me." (Psalm 16:6, NASB)

I do not know what kind of circumstances are besetting you today, but I am certain that watching people suffer is not a pleasant sight before the eyes of God. It is not His will that people to go through life carrying burdens of griefs and other hurdles that may cause them to feel and act in undesirable ways.

The Lord knows about our feelings and can help us to cope with our circumstances. He empathizes with our weaknesses and helps us through our difficulties. His Son Jesus descended from Heaven to give us an example of faith and dependence in the Almighty.

Jesus chose to depend on His Father to give us an example of what we need to do in the midst of our most critical situations. He also affirmed His followers with these encouraging words: "*I have given you an example, that you also should do just as I have done to you*" (John 13:15, ESV).

Certainly, Jesus showed us the ropes because He wanted us to know what to do whenever we felt overwhelmed by our troubling circumstances.

Appeal

Life could be like a bumpy ride uphill, in which troublesome situations could afflict our spirits and overwhelm our souls.

Nonetheless, the Almighty wants us to find peace and comfort in Him. He is always by our side. Therefore, we must lean in the Lord, trust, and praise always. He helps ease our burdens and brings solace to our broken hearts. He will show us what to do.

Remember these words of the Apostle: "*But, if any of you lacks wisdom, let him ask of God, who gives to all generously and without reproach, and it will be given him*" (James 1:5, NASB).

This means that we should ask God for wisdom to face your situations. He always knows what is best for everyone and will guide and show you the way. Therefore, take advantage of the Apostle's advice and discover the secret of staying strong amidst the distress. Keep your hopes up even in spite of your adversities and believe that the Lord is with you in the midst the chaos.

The Lord will mend your wounded heart. He will do it all because He loves you with an undying love that never fails. Therefore, do not feel broken, poor, lonely, abandoned or rejected. Remember that you belong to God, and this fact adds real value to your existence.

Hear His tender message of love: "*I have loved you with an everlasting love; therefore, I have drawn you with lovingkindness*" (Jeremiah 31:3, NASB). "*You are precious in my sight, since you are honored and I love you*" (Isaiah 43:4, NASB).

Yes! You are loved with a love that never ends. You are worthy and precious on His sight. Thus, you need to weep and crying your sorrows away no more. Think about these things whenever you feel overwhelmed and overtaken by difficulties. Whenever you feel lonely or afflicted, and whenever you do not know what else to do about your situations, remember that He is with you..

The Lord comes through for His servants as a Mighty Deliverer and will give them their breakthroughs. He is "our refuge and strength; a very present help in times of troubles" (Psalm 46:1, NASB).

The Lord will strengthen your soul. He will ease your pain, and help you find answers to your questions and bring closure to all your situations.

He can help you get through all your troubles and unwanted situations. Hence, come to the Lord in prayer, commit your ways onto Him, and trust Him, and He will help you out in the middle of your stormy situations.

The Lord will show you the way in which you should go. He will be your guiding counselor and will give you confident for triumphant living. Have you made Him the ruler of your heart?

"Finally, brothers and sisters, whatever is true, whatever is noble, whatever is right, whatever is pure, whatever is lovely, whatever is admirable --if anything is excellent or praiseworthy --think about such things."

- Philippians 4:8, NIV

APPENDIX

Works consulted:

The insights and information encompassed within the covers of this book, have their backbone on different sources related to the topic discussed herein. The themes discussed in this work have been inspired by past and present quotidian life experiences.

However, the author's personal insights have their backbone on numerous biblical references, and other creditable sources mentioned below.

1. Online Journal of Issues in Nursing, article name *Child Maltreatment: A Public Health Overview and Prevention Considerations,* by Melissa T. Merrick, PhD, and Natasha E. Latzman, https://www.ojin.nursingworld.org.
2. Medical News Today, article entitled *Everything You need To Know about Phobias,* by Christian Nordquist, https://www.medicalnewstoday.com.

We hope that these contents may contribute to nurturing your spirit and intellect. We also hope that that these contents may be a blessing to you and that in it, you may find all the tools you need to grow individual and collectively. May God continue to bless, help, and give you confident assurance for triumphant living.

"I can do all this through him who gives me strength."

- Philippians 4:13

MEET THE AUTHOR

YP Accilien is a Christian author, whose passion for writing compels her to write messages of hope and inspiration for today's world. She remains committed to deliver uplifting and inspirational content on every page of each book she writes aiming to make a difference in the lives of others.

YP has served as a Women's Ministry Leader in New Jersey, and as of today, she continues inspiring and motivating people through her public ministry as a speaker as well as a freelance writer.

In addition to buying her books, you can support YP by way of praying for her ministry, reading her literary works, and recommending them to other persons. To learn more about YP Accilien visit her website at www.memosandthings.com.

"But my God shall supply all your need according to his riches in glory by Christ Jesus."

- Philippians 4:19, KJV

BOOKS BY YP

Upcoming Titles

God Is With You, Book 2 – Ambassadors of Light, a faith-based guide, which delves in the subject of human relations at the light of God's purpose for people's lives as stated in the Bible.

Legado de Virtudes – A collection of stories, featuring different characters whose faith, valor, and altruistic demeanor helped them triumph over their difficulties.

"Rejoice in the Lord always; again I will say, rejoice!"

"Let your gentle spirit be known to all people. The Lord is near."

"Do not be anxious about anything, but in everything by prayer and pleading with thanksgiving let your requests be made known to God."

"And the peace of God, which surpasses all comprehension, will guard your hearts and minds in Christ Jesus."

- Philippians 4:4-7, NASB

BLURB ♦

God's with You is a nonfiction, faith-based, inspirational book, which addresses several issues typical of our quotidian living. These issues and situations are discussed in simple, but realistic manner. The book's chapters have been enriched with many practical examples and insightful suggestions to help individuals for triumphant living.

Contained within the covers of this book are several stories and anecdotes that can inspire and motivate readers to believe in a God that cares for the children of His creation.

There are also numerous biblical references that can empower, strengthen, and encourage individuals to withstanding the test of their circumstances. Readers who set out to embrace the positive stances recommended by the author of this book, are very likely to attain victory over their trials that may beset them as they travel through this sod.

"I have said these things to you, that in me you may have peace. In the world you will have tribulation. But take heart; I have overcome the world."

- John 16:33, ESV

www.ingramcontent.com/pod-product-compliance
Lightning Source LLC
LaVergne TN
LVHW091554060526
838200LV00036B/838